BWB Texts

Short books on big subjects from
great New Zealand writers

The Broken Estate

Journalism and
Democracy in a
Post-Truth World

MEL BUNCE

Published in 2019 by Bridget Williams Books Limited, PO Box 12474,
Wellington 6144, New Zealand, www.bwb.co.nz, info@bwb.co.nz.

ISBN 9780947518356 (Paperback), ISBN 9780947518363 (EPUB)
ISBN 9780947518370 (KINDLE), ISBN 9780947518387 (PDF)
DOI 10.7810/9780947518356

A catalogue record for this book is available from the National Library of
New Zealand. Kei te pātenga raraunga o Te Puna Mātauranga o Aotearoa te
whakarārangi o tēnei pukapuka

Acknowledgements
The publisher acknowledges the ongoing support provided by the Bridget
Williams Books Publishing Trust and Creative New Zealand.

Publisher: Tom Rennie
Editor: Barbara Graham
Cover and internal design: Neil Pardington Design
Typesetter: Tina Delceg
Printer: Printlink, Wellington

CONTENTS

*For the journalists –
and those who support them.*

INTRODUCTION

In one of the many low points of the 2016 US election campaign, a fake news story reported that Hillary Clinton was involved in a child sex ring run out of a pizza restaurant in Washington D.C. This conspiracy theory – 'Pizzagate', as it was inevitably called – started as a tweet on a white supremacist Twitter account. It was then repeated by fake news websites, ultra-right-wing commentators, and ultimately the mainstream media.

As the allegation spread, Comet Ping Pong – a real pizza restaurant and the supposed home of the trafficking ring – started to receive threats. The episode came to a dangerous climax when twenty-eight-year-old Edgar Welch went to the restaurant with a gun and opened fire, his shots hitting the walls and door.

Pizzagate was an extreme chapter in an extra-ordinary American election. But it was also a pivotal 'aha!' moment for media observers. The allegations against Clinton were fantastical, incendiary and based on zero evidence – but a remarkable number of people believed them. Reputable polls suggested that 33 per cent of Americans thought Clinton was 'probably' or 'definitely' involved in a child sex ring.[1] There was, essentially, no media outlet or institution that had the credibility to provide facts or dispel lies. The most industrialised country in the world, with the highest education levels in its history, had lost control of the truth.

As the US enters the 2020 election cycle, we still do not understand the ways in which social media, disinformation and online algorithms have fundamentally altered our information landscape. In New Zealand, the horrific terror attacks in Christchurch made us realise we are not insulated from the dark corners of the internet, where these falsehoods can breed radicalisation and violence.

In this information landscape, we need journalism more than we ever have before. We need trusted professionals to seek out the truth, verify claims, hold political leaders to account, and represent the diverse views of citizens. But, at exactly this moment, journalism is facing its own profound challenges – some of which are so extreme they threaten its survival. Journalists are under attack from creeping authoritarianism around the world – from Duterte in the Philippines, to Erdoğan in Turkey and Trump in the US. As the 2019 World Press Freedom Index concludes: 'The number of countries regarded as safe, where journalists can work in complete security, continues to decline, while authoritarian regimes continue to tighten their grip on the media.'[2]

Simultaneously, the economic foundations of the journalism industry appear to be breaking. Audiences are no longer willing to pay for news they can find online for free. And advertisers have stopped giving their money to the traditional news media, using Google and Facebook to reach potential customers instead. This advertising revenue was vital to the traditional journalism business model. Without it, news outlets are closing down and journalists are being laid off.

Journalism's economic crisis has hit New Zealand journalism particularly hard. We only spend a tiny amount of money on public media – far less per capita than Australia, the UK or Canada. This means less journalism protected from economic shocks. Meanwhile, our commercial news market is small, and owned – to an unusually large extent – by foreign investment groups. In print and online journalism, just two companies control 90 per cent of the New Zealand market. These companies have a legal, fiduciary obligation to make money for their international shareholders: they do not have a responsibility to the citizens of New Zealand or its democratic system. Faced with dwindling income, they have closed newspapers and cut the number of reporters they hire.[3]

The number of print journalists in New Zealand dropped by 61 per cent between the censuses in 2006 and 2013: from 2,214 down to 1,170.[4] This is an enormous decrease, even in the context of the global journalism crisis.[5] And while there are exciting new digital outlets doing some incredible reporting, the number of journalists they hire does not come close to replacing these losses.[6]

The journalists who remain are covering larger areas with fewer resources. In some corners, editors and managers are desperately trying to grow audience numbers, and the pressures to make sensational, attention-grabbing news have increased. Chris Barton, a former features writer at the *New Zealand Herald*, describes the 'tabloidisation' that started in the early 2000s, when newspaper circulation began slipping:

[M]otor accidents, any motor accident, suddenly became front page news. We were the *Car Crash Herald* ... My colleagues in features would mark off the trends of the day – women in bikinis, sharks and collisions. The perfect paper would have all three.[7]

It is easy to see these news stories and despair, to throw our hands up and criticise the state of the 'modern media' as a whole. But such sweeping generalisations are not constructive. They can foster cynicism about the entire journalism industry, at a time when it needs support more than ever.[8]

Sweeping criticisms of 'modern journalism' are not accurate, either. We had our fair share of dreadful journalism before the current crisis. News content in New Zealand – and around the world – was often dry, deferential to those with power, and almost monolithically white and male. There are endless historical examples of sensational news content, dumbed-down reporting, misinformation, and extremely partisan, party-political content.[9] Through much of the twentieth century, a small number of editors wielded enormous power as the gatekeepers to the public sphere, and they often used this for political and personal advantage.

Moreover – and somewhat confusingly – in some areas, journalism is better today than it ever has been. Even in 2016 – that nadir of global media and politics – there were amazing highs. The *Washington Post* and *New York Times* routinely published meticulously researched investigative journalism. Podcasting flourished, and even *Teen Vogue* started to do breakout political analysis. Chimamanda Ngozi Adichie, one of the great fiction writers of the twenty-first century, satirised the Trumps in a homage to Virginia Woolf,[10] while Ta-Nehisi Coates routinely dissected the legacy of slavery on modern race relations and politics.[11] And almost all of this content was online, freely available to anyone who wanted to look.

Cast the net around the New Zealand media and, in 2019, you can see some of the best journalism that has ever been made in this country. There are insightful analyses, cutting satirical websites, forensically documented investigations, and multimedia stories so ambitious and well executed they would be at home among Pulitzer Prize nominees.[12] Some news outlets are trying to make news with mass appeal, desperately chasing clicks to try to bring in digital advertising. But others have realised that, to make money, they will need to produce a quality product that people are willing to pay for.

As former editor of the *New Zealand Herald* Gavin Ellis puts it, '[t]here is an oasis of exceptionally good journalism in this country. Really exceptional work. But to have an oasis, you have to have a desert around it.'[13]

In this context, we need to ask more nuanced questions than 'is journalism in New Zealand good or bad?' We need to know exactly where its strengths and weaknesses lie. Are there areas where digital technology and new business models might help journalists do their work and hold elites to account? Where is journalism most at risk, and what can we do to protect it? And – more importantly, perhaps – what do we actually want from our news media? Whose views do we want it to platform and support?

I've been thinking about these questions for many years. My life has been entwined with the media, from my first job delivering newspapers around the cold morning suburbs of Dunedin, to my work now as a lecturer at a journalism school in London. As a child of the 1980s and 90s, I am among the last to grow up with ink on my hands. I learned about the world through the pages of the *Otago Daily Times*, the voices on Radio New Zealand, and the evening news. I assumed that the stories I encountered in the news were the most important issues on any given day.

After I got a job as a newspaper columnist and began researching the news industry, I learned the reality was much messier. Journalists are human, they have preferences and biases, and they work under huge pressures; for every story they report, there are hundreds that go untold. I became fascinated by the large, human-built chasm between the world we live in and its reflection in our media.

I wrote a dissertation on New Zealand newspaper reporting, and then went to the UK for more study. At Oxford, I focused my PhD on how journalists represented crises and conflict in Africa. In this work, I started to understand the power of media to shape lives. I read through the research on media effects, which shows that journalism can change minds, set the political agenda, frame the way people think about the world and move politicians to act. News stories can perpetuate oppression and fuel conflict, as well as bring down tyrants and bond communities together.

I'm now a researcher and lecturer in the Journalism Department at City, University of London, where we teach students from around the world. Working in London, I have a front row seat to the UK journalism industry, which is both dying and being reborn. I spend my days researching funding models and journalistic practices. As I learned more about the global media, and the challenges facing journalism, I wanted to explore these phenomena back home. Applying insights from these international studies and industry experiments to New Zealand would, I hope, offer some fresh perspective on our media sector.

Over several trips home, I spoke to a range of journalists, politicians and academics. I talked to editors and former editors of major newspapers, and journalists working across print, radio, TV and digital start-ups all around the country. I spoke with media commentators and researchers, and read through the work of New Zealand's talented media academics.[14] And I spent hours at the

National Library, poring through old newspapers and magazines, and documenting their evolution.

I learned about the ways that the internet and social media have broken journalism's traditional business model by untethering advertising from newspapers and unleashing huge quantities of poor information into the media ecosystem. Chapter 1 of this book looks at these twin crises of disinformation and financial collapse. Chapter 2 explores why this matters. Debates on the media often approach journalism as a partisan issue: with left- and right-wing pundits fighting over policy and government subsidies. But journalism is more fundamental than this. News and information are part of the scaffolding of democracy itself.[15] This chapter shows that, in a democracy, journalism has three key jobs: to provide trustworthy information; to hold those with power to account; and to provide a space for public debate.

Chapter 3 then looks at the state of New Zealand journalism today, asking whether it is performing these jobs. We see that, although there are pockets of journalistic excellence, there are also major, concerning gaps: whole geographic areas with no full-time journalists; important institutions that are not properly scrutinised; and groups that are poorly represented. The final chapter starts to imagine the future and asks how journalism can be rebuilt.

In my job we think a lot about how the industry is changing, and the skills that journalists will need to perform their role in the future. There are many things we don't know about how the media will evolve. But we know that credible journalism will always be essential, and that we must work hard to protect it.

1. 'WINTER IS COMING': A GLOBAL CRISIS IN JOURNALISM

In 2016, it became clear that traditional journalism was failing. In the three months before the US election, the most popular fabricated news stories had more likes, shares and comments on Facebook than the most popular, genuine articles from major news outlets.[1] And almost two out of three American adults reported that false news stories caused a great deal of confusion about the basic facts of current issues and events.[2]

Meanwhile, President Trump was waging a war on the mainstream media – the 'enemy of the people' – and he comfortably and prolifically lied, putting journalists in a difficult position. If they dismissed his claims, they were accused of bias. If they took them seriously, they did a disservice to the truth.

New York University Media Professor Jay Rosen

surveyed this media landscape in his 2016 article 'Winter is coming'. Noting the lack of resources for journalism, the decline and closure of hundreds of news outlets, the specific challenges of reporting on Trump, and the high distrust of almost every news organisation, Rosen concluded that '[f]or a free press as a check on power, now is the darkest time in American history since World War I'.[3]

In the UK that year, the Brexit referendum was also marred by widespread distrust in authorities and journalism. Capturing the mood of the times, George Osborne, then Chancellor of the Exchequer, announced that 'people have had enough of experts'. There was so much misinformation during the campaign that many still reject the outcome of the vote, fostering huge division around one of the most significant political decisions of a generation.

We are still unpacking the dramatic events of 2016. In particular, we are still learning about the foreign governments, private companies (like Cambridge Analytica) and political consultancies that tried to use the media for political gain. But one very clear lesson has emerged: technology has radically reshaped the information landscape, and journalism has not caught up. This reckoning has been coming for some time. For more than twenty-five years we have consumed information online. But we have rarely stopped to grapple with how this is changing our relationship with truth or authority. This chapter considers the two most urgent challenges facing journalism today: a crisis in trust, and a crisis in financing.

A CRISIS IN TRUST

In 2017, Collins Dictionary declared 'fake news' their Word of the Year. But most media researchers would prefer the phrase was removed from the English language and never seen again: it is very vague, and highly political.[4] The term is used to refer to everything from stories that are completely fabricated through to paid advertorials masquerading as journalism, opinion pieces, things taken out of context, and even satire.[5]

None of this content is new. There has always been false information: rumour, propaganda, sensationalist accounts, political lies and conspiracy theories. In the 1830s, for example, the *New York Sun* famously published a series of articles claiming that life had been discovered on the moon.[6]

But the internet has made the challenges of disinformation far more acute. It has led to the mass proliferation of information sources – both truthful and false – and the sheer quantity makes it increasingly difficult to sort fact from fiction. When celebrated British philosopher Onora O'Neill gave the 2002 Reith Lecture, she predicted the challenges to come:

It is quite clear that the very technologies that spread information so easily and efficiently are every bit as good at spreading misinformation and disinformation ... In spite of ample sources we may be left uncertain about the supposed evidence that certain drugs are risky, or that fluoride in the water harms, or that standards for environmental pollutants in water or air have been set too high (or too low or at the right level), that professional training of doctors or teachers are adequate or inadequate ... Proponents of views on these and countless other points may not heed available evidence and can mount loud and assertive campaigns for or against one or another position whether the available evidence goes for or against their views.[7]

This challenge cuts to the heart of some of our most dearly held ideals about free speech and democracy. For centuries, liberals have believed that open debate and discussion will help edge us closer to the truth. As John Milton argued in 1644, '[l]et [truth] and Falsehood grapple; who ever knew Truth put to the worse, in a free and open encounter?'[8] John Stuart Mill, perhaps the most famous advocate of free speech, made a similar argument. He suggested that, if we can only stand up and freely challenge false ideas, then we will see 'the clearer perception and livelier impression of truth, produced by its collision with error'.[9]

This central tenet is called into question by the chaos of online misinformation, channelled and amplified through social media. A recent massive study of online information flows published in *Science* analysed the spread of approximately 126,000 ideas across millions of tweets. It found that 'falsehood diffused significantly farther, faster, deeper and more broadly than truth in all categories of information'.[10] False news about politics spread particularly far: it reached more people faster and went deeper into their networks than any other category of false information.

According to a research project from Hunt Allcott and Matthew Gentzkow – economists based at NYU and Stanford, respectively – approximately half of those who saw fabricated political stories online in the US also believed them.[11] This is not, perhaps, surprising when we know that audiences struggle to fact check and verify sources online. The UK's Commission on Fake News and the Teaching of Critical Literacy Skills has run an experiment in schools and found that only 2 per cent of students have the critical literacy skills they need to tell if a news story is real or fake.[12] Two-thirds of teachers (60.9 per cent) believe fake news is increasing children's anxiety levels.

On the surface, fake news appears to be a technology-driven crisis. It is incredibly easy to set up a website, make it look like an official outlet, and share a fabricated article on social media. Alarmingly, the technology that enables such deception improves every day. Engineers and programmers have created software that can mimic voices exactly; and they are on the cusp of creating fake video from scratch that is indistinguishable from real footage. In the future, rather than reading a fake story stating that the Pope has endorsed Donald Trump for President, we will watch it with our own eyes.

Micah Gelman at the *Washington Post* calls this a 'dramatic game changer', noting that:

[W]e have never as a society faced ... the power of this fraud ... the power of it being something you can watch, with a voice and a face that is of a public figure saying something? Oh, I think this has massive potential to create all kinds of disruptions all over the world.[13]

One writer in *Atlantic* magazine has gone as far as arguing that 'manipulated video will ultimately destroy faith in our strongest remaining tether to the idea of a common reality'.[14]

Although it is exacerbated and spread on new technology, the 'fake news' crisis is not, at its core, a technological problem – it is a crisis of trust. When we have reliable sources that we trust to convey information and correct and challenge falsehood, then fabricated content does not cause the same damage. I was in the UK during the London riots in 2011. I remember watching on Twitter as absurd pieces of information swirled online. Some of these were terrible – like the claim that the police had attacked an unarmed girl. Others were comical – like the claim that protesters were breaking into the zoo to let out the animals, and rioters had taken over McDonalds to cook burgers. A study by researchers at the University of Manchester, working with the *Guardian*, has shown that, although these rumours were prevalent, they generally stopped spreading as soon as a 'trusted' Twitter user or authority figure questioned the evidence or rejected the claim.[15] Moreover, while the evening unfolded, it was possible to check the BBC website to see which rumours were confirmed.[16] In short, trusted individuals and institutions prevented these rumours spreading further.

The real challenge in the US in 2016 was not just social media or fake websites. It was that a huge portion of the population did not trust those in authority to tell them the truth. Political divisions were extremely high, and trust in politicians, the media and experts was at an all-time low. A poll from Gallup found that only 32 per cent of Americans had a 'fair' or 'great deal' of trust in the media. This had plummeted from the 1970s, when trust in the media was around 72 per cent. Most remarkably, only 14 per cent of Republicans said they had either a 'fair' or 'great deal' of trust in the media.[17]

In his book *Why Americans Hate the Media and How It Matters*, Jonathan Ladd documents the long-term drift toward this political polarisation, the diminishing common ground, and the more frequent and intense political attacks on the news media.[18] Ladd shows how major media outlets, battling for ratings and trying to differentiate their product in a large media market, became increasingly partisan and polemical. Rather than using arguments or evidence, commentators started to attack the morals and motives of their political opponents. If someone disagreed, they were simply a 'social justice warrior', or a 'heartless neo-con', and there was no need to engage with their actual ideas. John Ziegler, a conservative radio host in the US, voices his regret: 'Over the years, we've effectively brainwashed the core of our audience to distrust anything that they disagree with. And now it's gone too far because the gatekeepers have lost all credibility in the minds of consumers.'[19]

Beyond a few misguided stories here and there, New Zealand has not been particularly affected by misinformation. Our journalism is protected – somewhat ironically – because it is almost impossible to make money with audience clicks in New Zealand, regardless of whether a news story is true or fake (more on this, below). So we have been spared the interest of those who make fake news for commercial reasons. It is also because, as a small country in the south Pacific, we are, generally, of limited geopolitical interest to Russia and other countries that are 'leading' the world in sophisticated, targeted disinformation campaigns to undermine electoral processes and citizen trust in the media.[20] So we are largely spared from those who create disinformation for political reasons.[21]

Despite this, levels of trust in New Zealand journalism are still very low. The 2018 Acumen Edelman Trust Barometer surveyed 33,000 people around the world – including more than 1,000 people in New Zealand.[22] The survey breaks up the respondents into the 'informed public' (who follow current affairs closely) and the 'general public' (who do not). Globally, the proportion of the 'informed public' who said that they trusted the media to 'do what is right' was 53 per cent, while in New Zealand it was only 38 per cent. The global proportion of the 'general public' who trusted the media to 'do what is right' was 43 per cent, while in New Zealand it was a very low 31 per cent.

What's behind these low levels of trust in the media? Given the huge stakes involved, media and political scholars have started to pay this question a lot of attention.[23] Their initial work points to a range of factors, including political elites attacking the media. Somewhat ironically, elites and academics talking about the challenges of 'fake news' may be making the problem worse. Because when people hear the phrase 'fake news', they internalise the idea that the news is problematic, and that they cannot trust journalists (even the established, credible ones). In addition, there are a number of common journalistic practices that feed audience confusion, leaving people unsure who they can trust. One problematic practice is that news outlets commonly give a platform to views' that are widely discredited in an attempt to look 'balanced' and 'objective'. Through the 1990s and 2000s, for example, climate change denialists were often given an equal space in media debates, even though scientific consensus was extraordinarily high that the climate was changing.[24]

The problem of 'false balance', as it's sometimes called, has also become a significant problem for US journalists trying to report on President Trump. The President and his advisors frequently lie (or present 'alternative facts') and many outlets continue to present his lies alongside facts, as if the two have an equal chance of being right. Many believe this is having a significant, ongoing, polarising impact on the public sphere, pushing groups further and further apart, and decreasing the prospect of non-partisan cooperation.[25]

We do not have extreme partisanship in the New Zealand media, partly due to our small media market (few outlets can afford to exclude whole demographics from their potential audience). But we have seen a troubling related phenomenon: the blurring of lines between fact and opinion, particularly around climate reporting and other science topics. Mike Hosking, for example, one of the most well-known broadcasters in the country, argues that the overwhelming scientific consensus around climate change is political correctness. And, in 2014, he dismissed the views of thousands of scientists:

I'm afraid the IPCC – the International Panel on Climate Change – has issued its latest report ... The seas are rising, the storms are coming, the locusts are close, we are going to climatic hell in a handcart. That's of course, if you believe them. Which, as it turns out, I don't.[26]

The scientific community, in Hosking's view, is to be 'believed' or 'not believed'; it is an act of faith, rather than empiricism. This is a problematic direction of travel. If we don't trust in scientific methods or experts, then we start to question all sorts of evidence: why would we trust scientists when they tell us to vaccinate our children?

This slippage between reporting and opinion is especially common in personality-driven current affairs programming, which started in earnest in New Zealand in 1989, with the introduction of Paul Holmes' show, *Holmes*. The format is primarily designed to drive ratings, and it foregrounds opinion and punditry from hosts rather than the presentation of facts and evidence; such programming has been criticised from across the political spectrum and is particularly concerning when the commentators attack the scientific method itself, or the need for evidence in public policy.[27]

Sponsored content is another common and confusing journalistic practice that can blur the line between factual reporting and strategic content.[28] The most problematic form of this 'native advertising' (as it is sometimes called) is where an entire advert is made to resemble a news story. These are often labelled as 'advertorials' in such small font that it is common for audiences to believe it is 'genuine' news content. In a massive study of 7,800 young people's online behaviour, researchers at Stanford University found that 82 per cent of middle-schoolers could not distinguish between an advert labelled 'sponsored content' and a real news story appearing on a website.[29] The researchers concluded that, although these digital natives have a wealth of technical skills, they are just as easily duped as older test takers when it comes to evaluating information online.

The distinction between adverts and news can be particularly confusing when the platform companies (Facebook, Google and Twitter, for example) place adverts in the same location as promoted news stories. For example, if a user 'follows' a news organisation like the *Guardian*, and then the *Guardian* pays to promote one of their news stories, it can appear as an advert.[30] These practices have contributed to growing confusion about what media content is impartial information, and what is strategic content that has an agenda.

Alongside this confusion and a lack of trust, journalism is facing another, even more intense, crisis – one that threatens its very survival. This is a failure of the core business model.

AN (EXISTENTIAL) ECONOMIC CRISIS

It's easy to romanticise journalism – to celebrate its sacred role speaking truth to power. But, throughout history, most journalism has been made for a more mundane and self-interested reason: money. To understand why journalism looks the way it does, we must understand it as an economic product: who is covering the costs of news production, and what types of news do they value the most?[31]

Quality journalism is expensive to make, and audiences have almost never covered these costs in full. Instead, news outlets rely on alternative sources of income to subsidise their journalism: advertising, sponsorship, government funding, philanthropy and so on. Of these groups, advertisers have historically been the most important. In the US, advertising generates a massive 80 per cent of all income in the newspaper industry.[32] In New Zealand, this figure is estimated to be around 70 per cent.[33]

But the arrival of the internet gave advertisers

other options to reach audiences, and in the process it broke journalism's business model. Attracted by their reach, efficiency and incredible audience data, advertisers started giving their business to internet platforms rather than news outlets.[34] Google and Facebook alone now collect around 60 per cent of all digital advertising revenue in the US and the UK.[35] And industry watchers say the dominance of Google and Facebook in the advertising market is only intensifying: they have taken a staggering 99 per cent of recent growth.[36]

In New Zealand, Google and Facebook now take approximately 50 per cent of all digital advertising revenue.[37] Our media executives and news editors argue that Google and Facebook's domination of the advertising market make it incredibly difficult for any news outlet to profit from journalism.[38]

The internet killed another revenue source for newspapers: classified adverts. Once known by publishers as 'rivers of gold', this income dried up as people flocked to platforms like Trade Me and eBay. In 2000, US newspapers made US$19 billion from classified advertising; by 2012 this figure was only US$4.6 billion and steeply declining.[39]

The impact of these losses on frontline journalism has been brutal. Struggling to survive, news outlets fired journalists and massively increased the workload of those who remained. In the US in 1990, daily and weekly newspaper publishers employed about 455,000 reporters, clerks, salespeople, designers and the like. By January 2017, that same workforce was only 173,900.[40]

Circulation figures and advertising revenues continue to fall and the cuts to journalist numbers are not slowing down.[41]

Job cuts created a negative cycle – what some have rather dramatically called a 'death spiral'. Circulation decline led to advertising decline. Advertising decline led to cuts in editorial departments. Editorial cuts led to worse newspapers with less content. Worse newspapers led to fewer readers. With fewer readers, there was less income from advertising, which led to more cuts – and so on.[42]

Penny Abernathy, Professor of Journalism at the University of North Carolina, has meticulously detailed the ongoing cuts to the US news industry.[43] Her data shows that, over the last fifteen years, nearly 20 per cent of newspapers in the US have closed, and countless others have become shells – or 'ghosts' – of their former selves. An estimated 1,300 US communities have lost all their news coverage. This includes 200 counties that now have no newspaper at all, some of which hold significant governance, legal and administrative roles. In July 2019, Youngstown, Ohio – a city of 65,000 people in a larger metro area of 500,000 residents – became the first medium-sized US city to have no daily newspaper.[44]

Significantly, the people with the least access to local news are often the most vulnerable – the poorest, least educated and most isolated. James T. Hamilton, Director of the Journalism Program at Stanford University, has researched this issue and shown that income inequality directly generates information inequality. People with low incomes are less likely to be sought out by advertisers, less likely to spend money on subscriptions, less likely to vote, and less likely to connect with others online. These factors translate into less media content designed to capture their attention, aid their decision-making, or tell their stories.[45]

ONLINE JOURNALISM AS A SUBSTITUTE?

When news first moved online, many believed it would lead to a flourishing of journalism. They hoped that new start-ups, blogs and websites would take advantage of low overhead costs and contribute valuable information and critical perspectives to the public sphere.

Steven Waldman, who has written an influential overview of digital journalism in the US, lists its many positive contributions. He shows that news websites and blogs provide important original content, support a greater diversity of views, and have the potential to increase the reach, immediacy and engagement of news.[46] One of the major benefits of online journalism is that it supports cross-over exposure. Content made by one outlet can go viral, reaching audiences in other regions, groups and networks, unlike ever before – enriching the information and quality of debate across the public sphere.

To give one example, *Vice News Tonight* is a TV show aired on the cable channel HBO and specifically pitched at millennials. It has a (relatively) small regular audience of around 500,000. In August 2017, the outlet produced a special embedded report on white supremacists in Charlottesville, Virginia, during the 'Unite the Right' rally.[47] The video went viral online and was viewed more than 36 million times in its first week, making a major contribution to the mainstream conversation about race.

But these industry developments aside, online news sources simply have not replaced the work that was once done by (now closed down) offline outlets. First, because the number of new jobs in digital journalism has not kept pace with the jobs that have been (and continue to be) lost in news-paper journalism.

In the US, for example, the digital-native news sector grew from 7,400 newsroom employees in 2008 to about 13,000 in 2018. But this increase (around 6,000 jobs) fell far short of offsetting the loss of about 33,000 newspaper newsroom jobs.[48]

In New Zealand, there has similarly been a

drastic loss of journalism jobs in the print sector. These declined by 61 per cent between the censuses in 2006 and 2013, from a total of 2,214 down to 1,170.[49] The drop in the total number of journalists was much less stark taking into account the growth in digital journalism and online publishing, but it is still notable: 4,044 New Zealanders classified themselves as journalists in the 2006 Census, while in 2013 this figure was 3,603 – an 11 per cent decrease.

Moreover, the job growth in digital journalism is far from stable. Even the big global digital media companies like Buzzfeed, Vice and HuffPost face considerable financial challenges, and their journalists' jobs are precarious. In 2019, these companies cut 2,000 jobs from their teams, and the New Zealand office of Vice closed down. Other websites that were previously hailed as digital success stories – like The Pool (a UK website aimed at women) and Mic (a millennial news site specialising in social justice stories) – have either closed or reduced their news teams.

In New Zealand, there are a number of new and exciting digital publications, like *Newsroom* and *The Spinoff*. These outlets have rapidly achieved credibility in the eyes of the industry, scoring scoops and winning prizes. In the 2019 Voyager Media Awards, *The Spinoff* won Website of the Year, and *Newsroom*'s Melanie Reid won Best Reporter (among other prizes for both).

However, they do not – as of yet – publish a full news offering. *The Spinoff*, for example, primarily publishes analysis and feature journalism, focusing on topics like politics, media, TV and culture.[50] The website content is diverse, ranging from major documentaries about home ownership and political analyses through to summaries of the TV show *The Bachelor* and definitive rankings of chip brands. But the outlet does not produce day-to-day news reports (and nor does it aspire to). *The Spinoff* editor Toby Manhire says:

Ultimately, the model is not the solution for public news journalism.... My view about *The Spinoff* is that it's complementary, in the way that a news magazine or a feature magazine can be ... I think it would be disingenuous to suggest the success of *The Spinoff* means the news media is fine, because we don't really do news.[51]

Another limitation of new digital media outlets is that their employees tend to be clustered in urban areas. In the US, for example, 73 per cent of all internet publishing jobs are concentrated in corridors on the east and west coasts. The remaining 27 per cent are spread across the entire country, and that includes major metropolitan areas, such as Houston and Chicago.[52] In New Zealand, the new ventures like *Newsroom* and *The Spinoff* are based in Auckland and Wellington. One promising exception is *Crux*, a new start-up covering the Queenstown district, and structured as a trust.[53]

There are also countless, amateur-run websites, some of which focus on providing community information and news and have been described as a form of 'hyperlocal journalism'. This is a fairly nebulous term used to refer to everything from an online newsletter from the local rugby club through to a more established, sophisticated site collecting news and comments.

Many of these websites publish quality information and, in some instances, do the work that local papers did in the past.[54]

But they also have limitations. One is that they are often run with very precarious income streams – indeed, most have no income at all.[55] And they are usually run by just one or two people who spend fewer than ten hours working on their site per week.[56] This means these websites can rarely cover the day-to-day events in a community. They may also stop altogether when, for example, the main author is on holiday, sick or busy.[57]

Some have also questioned the quality of the content on hyperlocal sites. In the UK, media researcher Andy Williams and colleagues analysed 1,941 posts from 313 hyperlocal sites,[58] finding that, while there was some good content, much was 'partial, amateurish and trouble-making or just descriptive, banal and mundane'.[59] Importantly, the hyperlocal sites, usually run by citizens without journalistic training, did not tend to use sources to verify their reports: only half of the posts cited any sources at all.[60]

This is not intended to criticise hyperlocals, which can contribute to information sharing and community building. It is simply to say that, in their current form, they are not replacing the local journalism that once existed in these communities. As a report from Carina Tenor, a media researcher at the London School of Economics, concluded:

There might be some local exceptions, but on the whole, it is unlikely that the resources to perform accountable journalism or to act as a Fourth Estate will ever become comparable to traditional media.[61]

Studies have reached similar conclusions in the US and Sweden, where researchers describe local sites as 'imperfect substitutes at best for most newspapers when it comes to local government coverage'.[62]

IS ANYTHING WORKING?

There is no obvious replacement for the huge revenue that was brought in by advertising and has long subsidised public interest reporting. Clay Shirky, the internet analyst, argues that it is highly unlikely any one business model will be able to replace the lost revenue from advertising.[63]

However, there are some areas where experimentations are succeeding. A small number of outlets – usually very big ones – are having success with online subscriptions. The *New York Times* and *Washington Post* have grown their audiences enormously, and are investing their subscriptions back into journalism, hiring new editorial staff and increasing coverage.[64] These two mega outlets, like the *Guardian*, benefit from enormous economies of scale: they pursue and reach audiences around the globe. Other groups having success with subscriptions include *De Correspondent*, which was launched in the Netherlands, with global supporters; and Amedia, which owns a network of news outlets in Norway (a country with very high levels of newspaper readership, and a strong tradition of paying for community news).

Financial newspapers like the *Wall Street Journal* and *Financial Times* are also having success building an online subscription model. These outlets operate in a quite different market from the one for general news. Business news readers appear to 'enjoy' paying for their news, because it makes the information more scarce, increasing its value (and potentially giving them an edge over the competition).[65] Moreover, many workplaces pay for subscriptions to these outlets, and advertisers are willing to pay greater sums to reach their audience, who tend to be in a higher income bracket.[66]

The subscription model is much more challenging for small to medium outlets that report general news. Mark Thompson, chief executive of the *New York Times*, believes there will be a 'bloodbath' in the coming years as even more mid-sized newspapers are obliterated during the transition to digital. Thompson, previously the director-general of the BBC, even suggests that '[i]n the US it may be that only two or three titles survive, other than specialists'.[67]

The main challenge is, of course, that audiences are highly accustomed to getting information and news online for free, and most are not willing to pay. Researchers at the Reuters Institute for the Study of Journalism at Oxford University commission an annual survey of news consumers around the world – the *Digital News Report*. Their 2019 results showed that, on average, only 11 per cent of respondents had paid for news in the past year – a figure that has barely changed since the statistics were first collected in 2013. Moreover, those who do pay are usually only willing to pay for one subscription.[68]

There are some small glimmers of hope within the survey data, however. First, the percentage of people willing to pay has increased in some countries. In the US, the so-called 'Trump-bump' led to a 7 per cent increase in the portion of people paying for the news, up to 16 per cent. Some of this is transactional: audiences have become more engaged with politics and they want access to news content that is behind paywalls. For others this is a charitable act – a desire to support the media, even where they can access the content for free. The most notable example of this is the *Guardian*'s membership model; some podcasts are also succeeding as a result of membership donations.

A second reason for (very cautious) hope is that young people appear more willing to pay for online media content than older consumers. On average, across all thirty-eight countries surveyed in the *Digital News Report*, the group most willing to pay for online news is the twenty-five to thirty-four demographic.[69] This partly reflects the fact that older age groups are still paying for print journalism and TV packages. But it may also reflect the fact that younger consumers have become accustomed to paying for media content on platforms like Spotify, Netflix and iTunes.[70] As these consumers age, and with ever more online content monetised through a variety of pay models, the hope is that the 'culture of free' will erode.

Some outlets are succeeding through philan-thropic support and charity, alongside their commercial revenues. Foundations, rich elites and businesses have long subsidised and funded news outlets for strategic, political or philanthropic reasons.[71] In the US, Amazon's Jeff Bezos owns the *Washington Post*. And billionaire Patrick Soon-Shiong has recently purchased the *Los Angeles Times*, which he plans to build into an 'institutional public trust in a private setting', akin to Harvard or Stanford.[72] His deep pockets mean that he can take a long-term view, and give the paper the much needed time and space to experiment with content and revenue strategies – as he told one interviewer, 'I'm looking at a hundred year plan, literally.'[73] Philanthropist Graeme Wood stepped in to support the *Guardian*'s expansion into Australia, agreeing to fund it for two years and wipe the debt if the outlet failed.[74]

Google and Facebook have also recently pledged large funds to support journalism. Google pledged US$350 million over three years for its 'News Initiative' to combat misinformation and help media outlets monetise news content. In January 2019, Facebook announced its own US$300 million support for US journalism projects, which includes a particular focus on supporting local news.[75] This funding has been greeted with cynicism by some in the news industry, who believe the platforms are trying to mitigate bad press (particularly in the case of Facebook) and ward off the spectre of government regulation. Others have pointed out that Google funding is designed to convince newsrooms to use the company's products.[76] But most newsrooms are willing to take support where they find it. As of yet, these platforms have not been used to support New Zealand outlets or journalists.[77]

Individual journalists and small outlets are also having some limited success generating funding from the public, using intermediaries such as Patreon, New Zealand's PressPatron, and other crowdfunding platforms.

Finally, there are a number of social enterprises making things work. In the US, Elizabeth Green has set up the not-for-profit outlet Chalkbeat, building it into a team of thirty who report on education in seven states, paid for by sponsors and readers. Green, who is also the cofounder of the American Journalism Project, which hopes to scale this model, draws an analogy with the performing arts:

The tickets I buy to see my local ballet make up well under a third of what it actually costs to produce this moving art. The rest of the dance sector's costs are covered through donations, corporate sponsorships, and creative commercial sources beyond tickets, like intellectual property licenses, educational services, and merchandising.[78]

The non-profit *Texas Tribune* is another success story. Founded by a group of journalists and the philanthropist and venture capitalist John Thornton, the *Tribune* is now a nearly US$10 million operation, paid for by an impressively diversified set of revenue streams: donations, philanthropists and grants from media support organisations like the Knight Foundation.

So, there are some places where journalism is surviving – and even thriving – online. These success stories suggest that outlets may find it easier to monetise their online journalism when:

- they are global in scope, and can benefit from economies of scale and/or a large potential audience, as in the case of the *New York Times* or *Washington Post*
- they target rich audiences or business professionals
- their audience is politically motivated, or passionate about a niche topic
- they are based in countries (like Norway) where there is an extremely high level of newspaper readership, and high portions of the population are willing to pay for the news[79]
- they have diverse revenue flows that might include donors, membership schemes, sponsors, adverts and side businesses (such as events companies cr consultancy projects).

Strikingly, however, there are very limited examples of commercial success stories for organisations that are making online local news – the area of journalism most negatively affected by digital disruption. As Emily Ramshaw, the Editor in Chief at the *Texas Tribune*, comments:

[T]here are some folks who are stepping in to try to bail out these news organisations and ... treat them as philanthropic endeavours ... [but] I'm very, very scared and pessimistic about what happens with these regional dailies because there really isn't anything in place to ... pick up the slack when and if those folk shutter ... I'm very afraid what's going to happen in these communities.[80]

CONCLUSION

This chapter has outlined some of the very real and pressing threats that the journalism industry faces in 2019. This includes, first, a widespread crisis in trust, where audiences around the world are unsure which information sources they can rely on. The second is a major rupture in the journalism business model: it is incredibly difficult for news outlets to make money in the digital age. The next section asks: why does this matter?

2. WHY DO WE NEED JOURNALISM?

Why should we care about the crises facing journalism? It's common to hear journalism called 'the fourth estate': an institution that is necessary for democracy to function. But what does this actually mean?

Pippa Norris, a celebrated political scientist who spends her time between Harvard and Sydney universities, answers this question by going back to first principles. Drawing on theories of representative democracy developed by Joseph Schumpeter and Robert Dahl, she argues that journalism has three key roles. It is a *mobilising agent* for public learning and participation (so that citizens have the information they need to vote); it is a *watchdog* against the abuse of power (so that civil liberties are protected and bad behaviour can be voted out); and it provides a *civic forum* for debate, which acts as a conduit between citizens and those who represent them.[1] If journalism does not perform these tasks, then the democratic system itself is at risk. This chapter introduces these three principles, showing just how big the stakes are.

TRUSTWORTHY INFORMATION

The media's first job in a democracy, according to Norris, is to provide trustworthy information about public issues. For countries to hold meaningful elections, citizens need to know what is happening. What are the big issues? How are different groups suggesting these are addressed? Are government interventions working? Without this information, Norris argues, we cannot make informed votes, and the democratic process becomes meaningless.[2]

Barbara Kingsolver captures this idea in her novel *The Poisonwood Bible*, set in the newly formed Democratic Republic of Congo. In the outer reaches of the country, the Congolese have not heard of the country's upcoming election; they do not know the people running for office, or how the outcome may affect their lives. Nonetheless, an official turns up and asks them to vote by putting pebbles in baskets representing candidates. The process is surreal and absurd – without knowing what the candidates stand for, the vote cannot be meaningful.

As newspapers around the world close down, we see the real, democratic challenges facing communities that do not have access to news and information. Rachel Howells, a media researcher in the UK, has written a PhD on the Welsh town Port Talbot, for example, where the sole news outlet closed down. Her extensive, in-depth examination found that the town suffered from a deep 'democratic deficit' after the closure:

I found evidence for confusion, lack of fore-knowledge of the issues before official decisions about them were final, frustration, powerlessness, speculation, rumour, and numerous experiences of opaque public institutions that are perceived not to give adequate access to information.[3]

Journalism doesn't just give citizens the knowledge they need to vote, it also gives them a reason to care. Ronald Heifetz, Senior Lecturer at Harvard Kennedy School, describes a newspaper as 'an anchor', because it 'reminds a community every day of its collective identity, the stake we have in one another and the lessons of our history'.[4] Or, as Benedict Anderson famously argued, the media helps to create 'imagined communities', providing a shared language and reference points that bring us closer to our fellow citizens.[5]

Journalism helps people define and maintain neighbourhoods in large cities, and it can bring people together across sparsely populated, rural areas. Large research studies show that this matters to levels of political engagement: communities with news outlets tend to have higher voter turnout compared with communities that do not, even when other factors are controlled for.[6]

Of course, not all journalism is created equal. Some forms of reporting are much more valuable in creating an informed citizenry. Academics and media commentators are often fiercely critical of what they see as 'dumbed-down' journalism, and a rise in 'soft news' about celebrities and human interest. They argue that this 'tabloid' journalism is deeply problematic as it does not inform the audience, and it can over-simplify complex issues.

We need to be careful when making these criticisms, however. In my own research, I've looked at how softer feature reporting about Africa can engage audiences in a way that hard news does not.[7] 'Hard' political and humanitarian news about Africa often focuses on conflict and crises, suffering and corruption. These stories are extremely important, but generally attract a very small audience of 'serious' news consumers. A 'soft' human interest story, by contrast, can reach a large audience and inform them indirectly.

One foreign correspondent I interviewed gave the example of a feature story he'd written about a gorilla in Uganda that had its own Facebook page. This story did not inform the reader about the political situation in Uganda. But it did attract a large audience, and it showed them a wired-up, tech-savvy corner of the continent that they likely were unfamiliar with. This is not a small thing. As well-known Africanist James Ferguson points out, audiences in the West tend to perceive Africa as a 'shadow' – a space that technology and innovation have not reached. News content can challenge these stereotypes and create more positive associations.[8] The article also brought to the attention of its readers important conservation issues for the endangered species.[9]

Swedish media scholars Henrik Örnebring and Anna Maria Jönsson have also shown that journalism considered 'bad' in its own time often has the potential to serve the public good just as much as 'respectable journalism':

From the very beginning, the tabloid press was criticised for sensationalism and emotionalism, for over-simplification of complex issues, for catering to the lowest common denominator and sometimes for outright lies. But tabloid journalism also managed to attract new publics, by speaking to them about issues previously ignored, in new, clearly understandable ways.[10]

One example of this was the 'yellow journalism' that became popular in the US at the end of the nineteenth century. Joseph Pulitzer, a pioneer of the genre, was fond of sensational headlines and ardent campaigns. His journalism often stretched the truth, but it also raised awareness of important issues such as sub-standard housing and the treatment of immigrants. This journalism engaged working-class readers who had historically been excluded from the public sphere.[11]

W. T. Stead pioneered similar sensational journalism in the UK. This included, most famously, an exposé on child prostitution and trafficking in London. Stead went undercover and 'purchased' a thirteen-year-old girl to show how easy it was. His reporting was widely condemned by elites (as well as vigorously purchased by them!), who described it as immoral, repugnant and unjustified; he was even thrown in prison. But his reporting led to the Criminal Law Amendment Act of 1885, which raised the age of consent for girls from thirteen to sixteen.[12]

Moreover, journalistic conventions that are considered 'bad' at one point in history can become perfectly acceptable in another. One clear example of this is the interview. Today, interviews are among the most common method used by journalists to gather information. But in the nineteenth century, European journalists thought that interviewing was a crass American invention – a sensational attempt to put elites on the spot and try to 'catch them out'. They were considered an impertinent and aggressive invasion of privacy.[13]

To be clear, tabloid news content can be deeply problematic; it can dumb down issues and mislead people. But those of us who are passionate about journalism have to remember that most of the population is not. Stories that can engage large audiences and expose them to important ideas can therefore make an important contribution to creating an informed citizenry. 'Soft' news is not inherently bad, nor playful, personal or even funny news (provided it's true).[14]

WATCHDOG OF THE POWERFUL

The media's second job in a democracy, according to Norris, is its most famous: to act as a watchdog of the powerful. Governments around the world have long relied on journalists to do this work. When the Founding Fathers deliberated on how to govern the United States, Thomas Jefferson argued that a critical press must be the very first institution, from which the others would follow: 'were it left to me to decide whether we should have a government without newspapers or newspapers without a government, I should not hesitate a moment to prefer the latter.'[15] Without newspapers, Jefferson reasoned, there would be an unacceptable disconnect between the work of the government and the people they represented. He had no doubt that, should this gap emerge, those in charge would abuse their power and rule for personal gain. Without scrutiny, leaders can ignore the rights of citizens and the rule of law: democracy itself can be at risk. Indeed, democracy and journalism are so intertwined, argued media critic James Carey, that they are essentially 'names for the same thing': neither exists without the other.[16] This is why authoritarian regimes so frequently target and undermine journalists; and it is why Yale University historian Timothy Snyder is so concerned about recent attacks on journalism in the US: 'post-fact', he argues, 'is pre-Fascism'.[17]

We tend to associate investigative journalism with its most celebrated practitioners: Bob Woodward and Carl Bernstein at the *Washington Post,* for example, whose Watergate investigation led to the resignation of President Nixon; the *Spotlight* team who revealed the Catholic Church's extensive cover-ups of child abuse. Or Seymour Hersh, who uncovered the US army's massacre of civilians at My Lai during the Vietnam War, as well as the degrading treatment of detainees in Abu Ghraib prison some four decades later. These are the pieces of investigative journalism so significant that they changed the shape of US history, reforming the offices of President, church and army. They uncovered life-and-death abuses of power that no other institution or person was able or willing to stop.

But investigative journalism also involves much more mundane work. It includes monitoring the day-to-day exercise of power at all levels of society, and asking questions like, which businesses are awarded government contracts? Do prisons and schools deliver quality services? Are environmental regulations followed? These are the nuts and bolts of daily governance, and they shape our lives as citizens. Although these questions appear pedestrian, they can have life-and-death consequences.

In 2017, a horrific fire in London's Grenfell Tower killed more than seventy people. Many have argued that, with greater journalistic scrutiny, the tragedy may have been averted.[18] The risk of a catastrophic fire on the estate had been raised in local council meetings and flagged up with eerily prophetic words by the Grenfell Action Group, who noted the lack of tested fire safety equipment and access issues. Historically, there were journalists assigned to attend these council meetings, ask questions and follow up on resident concerns. But these positions have all but disappeared in recent years, as local news production in the UK has shrunk.[19]

Of course, we cannot know the difference that more scrutiny might have made. But we do know that the mere presence of a journalist at a council meeting can change how officials behave, making them more cognisant of citizen concerns and potential criticism. As MIT media researcher Ethan Zuckerman argues:

Only a few dozen people might read the minutes of last night's meeting at City Hall, but it matters immensely that a seasoned political reporter is scanning those notes carefully, looking for possible scandals or abuse and threatening to splash them on the front page, if officials don't behave ethically.[20]

As well as holding power to account, investigative journalism makes government vastly more efficient. In *Democracy's Detectives*, James T. Hamilton, Director of the Journalism Program at Stanford University and an economist by training, has analysed the impact of 10,000 pieces of investigative journalism in the US. He found that 6 per cent of stories led to a resignation, 4 per cent to indictments, 3 per cent to firings, and 1 per cent to new laws. These investigations minimised corruption, ensured that competent people were running public services, and made public bodies more efficient. To give just one example, an investigative series on the probation system in North Carolina led to a change in personnel, law, policies and state spending. Hamilton estimates that for each dollar the newsroom spent on the investigation, there was US$287 in net policy benefits to the state during the first year of the reforms alone.[21]

The impact on law and government is why investigative journalism is sometimes referred to as the 'first draft of legislation', says James Hollings, Head of Journalism at Massey University.[22] Hollings gives the example of Matt Nippert's work at the *New Zealand Herald*, which has drawn attention to transnational corporations that don't pay taxes, prompting government action – and savings. Another example (of many) is the work that Paula Penfold did at the now defunct current affairs show *3D*. In one investigation, her team showed Stephen Wilce, former Chief Scientist at the Ministry of Defence, with one of the highest possible levels of security clearance, as a fantasist. Wilce had applied for the job with an embellished CV, and he later made claims to colleagues about being a Royal Marine and a member of the British Olympic bobsleigh team.[23] As a result of the investigation, Wilce resigned. An inquiry subsequently found that the Ministry had failed to run appropriate checks, and recommended that the vetting processes were reformed – the journalists essentially did the government's due diligence for them.[24]

Beyond the government, journalists also scrutinise businesses and corporations, protecting consumer rights and making sure that companies comply with regulations. Research in the US, by economist Pamela Campa, has shown that the mere presence of a newspaper in a town can reduce the amount of pollution from local oil or gas companies. She found that there was, generally speaking, very little news coverage of oil and gas plants in US local newspaper reports: only 4 per cent of the top twenty polluters in each state received any coverage at all. But when there was news coverage, its impact on emissions was dramatic. In some cases, reporting led to a 29 per cent reduction in emissions compared to plants that did not receive news coverage. Without the presence of these 'night-watchers', Campa argues, corporations are free to pollute without scrutiny.[25]

PUBLIC SPHERE FOR DEBATE

The media's third and final job is to provide a platform for debate: what Norris calls a 'civic forum'. The media is a place where citizens can voice their concerns and, ideally, debate policy solutions.

The idea of the media as a public sphere has a long history, and is most famously associated with Jürgen Habermas, who argued that democracy required a space 'outside the control of the state, where citizens could debate the important issues of the day'.[26] Habermas believed the European coffee shops and salons in the eighteenth century served this function: they brought citizens together to identify and debate public issues. Scholars have since pointed out that Habermas was romanticising the eighteenth-century saloons and coffee shops. Their customers – almost uniformly rich, white men – were just as likely gossiping about palace intrigue as they were debating public policy. But his argument has had a lasting impact by describing a state to which we should aspire.

In all states, citizens need to make difficult decisions about shared resources. Who should pay to protect the environment? Should the council prioritise its spending on the library or the rugby stadium? In a representative democracy, we elect leaders to make these decisions on our behalf. But one vote every three years is a blunt tool: it provides limited insight into citizen values and priorities. The media is one of the few channels through which citizens can air and debate issues as they arise.

Newspapers in New Zealand have played this role since its days as a British colony. Like Habermas' European coffee shops, New Zealand's early newspapers tended to represent the views of (relatively) privileged, white men. They captured the desire of this group for self-government and, as these newspapers were circulated around elites in the UK, helped to build the case for independence.[27] These early newspapers paid far less attention to the opinion and experience of the Māori population already in New Zealand. Indeed, they often published highly stereotypical and negative representations of Māori. Researcher Matthew Nickless argues these representations helped to justify land grabs in the early days of the colony.[28]

Today news outlets continue to provide a vital space to express views and hold public debates. And there is evidence that – for better or worse – politicians today continue to listen and respond to news coverage. In the international arena, this has been referred to as the 'CNN effect', where extensive news coverage of an issue can, *on occasion*, prompt officials to change their foreign policy.[29] Domestically, there is ample evidence that media coverage can make politicians (and civil servants) prioritise some issues and solutions over others. Moreover, studies show that issues that receive extended coverage in the media are often seen by audiences as the most important issues of the day – a phenomenon known as 'agenda setting'. News coverage takes some issues and makes them more salient – the housing crisis, for example, or clean water – and this creates pressure on the government to act. The flip side of this is that issues that are ignored are less likely to be addressed.[30]

In some instances (but certainly not all) the news media can help audiences reach compromise. Studies from the US have shown that, when news outlets close down, levels of political polarisation increase. One manifestation of this is that voters become less likely to 'split their vote' between candidates from different political parties.[31]

Because of the influence of the news media – on both politicians and citizens – it's crucial that it represents our community, rather than simply providing a platform for the elite and powerful. If we strive for a democracy where the government works for the majority, not the minority, then we need our media to reflect the full diversity of the population and their varying concerns. We need to hear from farmers as well as environmentalists, landlords and house owners as well as renters. As New Zealand political scientist Richard Mulgan writes:

[T]he media should provide a forum, or set of forums, in which all competing points of view can be debated and in which everyone can have a fair chance of contributing to the formation of public policy.[32]

This is an ideal, of course, but it is an important one to strive for. And it is one at which news organisations commonly fail. Around the world, journalism often does a poor job of representing minority groups. This includes, but is certainly not limited to, LGBT+ groups,[33] those with health conditions and disabilities,[34] refugees and immigrants, racial and religious minorities,[35] and many more. News coverage of these groups is often marginalised, stereotypical and overwhelmingly negative.

This negative and prejudiced media content matters enormously. Scholars have shown there is a 'priming' effect whereby stereotypical reporting can prompt and reinforce prejudice. In one important study, a group of participants were shown a TV comedy skit that included stereotyped portrayals of black people. Another group were shown neutral TV clips. Both groups were then given details of an incident involving a black student accused of assault. The white participants who had earlier viewed the stereotyped clip were more likely to assume that the black student was guilty of assault. The authors argue that exposure to racial stereotypes makes a white viewer more aware of the differences between themselves and the black 'other' being depicted. They are then more likely to perceive them as a threat or as a criminal.[36]

This depressing finding has been confirmed by many consequent studies. Elizabeth Levy Paluck, a Psychology Professor at Princeton University and a MacArthur 'Genius Grant' winner, has added important nuance to our understanding. In one project, she conducted a large-scale experiment using a radio show in Rwanda, where there are still many tensions between the Hutu and Tutsi ethnic groups following the 1994 genocide. In her study, one group were exposed to a soap opera that featured an inter-ethnic love story. Meanwhile, a control group were shown a neutral public health programme. Paluck found that the people who listened to the soap opera did not change their beliefs about inter-ethnic relationships. But –

fascinatingly, and importantly – they did change their behaviour. In focus groups, those who had seen the soap opera were less likely to say inflammatory things about the other ethnic group, and they became more likely to seek inclusive solutions to problems. Paluck argues that this is because exposure to the soap opera changed what the listeners thought were the prevailing social norms, and this changed what they considered appropriate to say out loud. Put another way, we learn what's 'normal' through the media (as well as from our peers, schooling, the law and so on).

CONCLUSION

This chapter has shown the vital role that journalism plays in a democracy – collecting and verifying information, holding elites to account, and providing a forum for debate. The next chapter uses these principles as 'measuring sticks' and asks how New Zealand journalism is performing: where is the news succeeding, and where is it most at risk?

3. JOURNALISM IN
NEW ZEALAND

New Zealand has been hit particularly hard by the economic crisis facing journalism. We are affected by all of the same deep cuts in journalism that other industrialised countries are experiencing. Circulation and advertising revenue are falling, and digital revenue has not replaced it. In addition to these, we have a number of our own specific challenges.

Roy Greenslade, a former newspaper editor in the UK, has been a media commentator for more than two decades. In the early 2000s, he visited New Zealand, surveyed the size of the news industry and the concentration of ownership, and declared that 'the situation for newsprint and publishers was direr than anywhere else in the English-speaking world'.[1]

Greenslade's pessimism hinges on several factors. The first challenge is the small size of our media market. Quality journalism costs a lot to make, and these costs remain reasonably fixed no matter how many people read, watch or listen to a news item. This creates what economists call 'economies of scale', and it gives news outlets with large audiences a very big advantage.[2] With only 4.7 million people in New Zealand, there is a hard limit to how much money can be made from cover sales, digital subscriptions or advertising.[3]

The US, with a population of 323 million people, can sustain all manner of weird and wonderful niche products at a national level, from shows about military spending and healthcare, to an entire week of programmes about sharks.[4] Importantly, there is a big enough population to support at least some high-quality, public interest journalism at the national level – outlets like the *Atlantic*, *New Yorker* and *New York Times* that do extensive reporting and analysis. Even if only 1 per cent of the population are willing to pay for this content, that still amounts to 3.2 million customers.

New Zealand's second challenge is isolation, which means we cannot easily share news content or production costs with neighbouring countries. The population of Ireland is almost identical in size to New Zealand. But at the last count, the Irish Republic had eight national newspapers as well as numerous metro, regional and local papers: far more than New Zealand. Their journalists are also less pressured. A global study called the Worlds of Journalism project periodically surveys international journalists. In the most recent survey, 89.3 per cent of New Zealand journalists said that the 'profit-making' pressure on their work had increased. In Ireland, by comparison, this figure was only 68.8 per cent.[5] One of the key reasons for this is that the big newspapers in the UK – *The Times*, the *Daily Mail* and so on – publish Irish editions. These papers have core content that is shared across the British Isles (sports, world news, arts and culture, and so on), which drastically reduces the cost of producing the paper from scratch. This shared content is then supplemented with original, Ireland-specific reporting on politics and social issues.

OWNERSHIP

A third major challenge for New Zealand relates to ownership. The majority of our news outlets are owned by a small handful of international, profit-driven companies. There are key public providers – Radio New Zealand, Māori Television, and government-owned TVNZ. But outside these, as Thomas Owen, a Senior Lecturer at Auckland University of Technology, writes, 'our overall mainstream media ecology is dominated by transnational, financialized, short-term corporate investors'.[6]

This landscape has been meticulously documented by Merja Myllylahti, who for the last several years has authored the New Zealand Media Ownership Report on behalf of the AUT Centre for Journalism, Media and Democracy. In the 2016 report, Myllylahti concluded that New Zealand is one of the most globalised, commercially driven media spheres in the world.[7] The 2017 and 2018 reports find the pattern unchanged, although there had been a small increase in independent providers online.[8]

The lack of independent, locally owned media means that New Zealand only scores 4/10 on the Bertelsmann Stiftung Foundation's 'Sustainable Governance Indicators', which examine media ownership and pluralism around the world. Many countries the same size as New Zealand score considerably higher: Ireland was awarded 8/10, Denmark, Norway and Sweden 9/10, and Finland 10/10.[9]

The three biggest media groups – Stuff, NZME and MediaWorks – own the majority of news outlets in New Zealand. And these three groups are largely owned by international financial institutions: banks, hedge funds and investment managers.[10] These groups are a world away from the individuals, families and businesses that historically owned news outlets and tended to have a direct involvement in the community on which they reported.[11] Rather, they are foreign institutions that have a legal, fiduciary obligation to make profit for their shareholders.[12]

Researchers have repeatedly demonstrated that, over time, media companies owned by financial institutions tend to cut the amount they spend on their journalism in order to maximise their profits. Abernathy argues that this ownership model is directly responsible for the 'news deserts' that have emerged across the US.[13] Many industry analysts and researchers agree, providing evidence from around the world. In Canada, the biggest newspaper group is controlled by two US hedge funds that specialise in buying so-called 'distressed-debt' companies. To profit from these faltering businesses, they slash costs, suck out cash flow and sell off assets for scrap. Martin Langeveld, an industry expert at Harvard University's Nieman Journalism Lab, describes the strategy as 'cannibalizing' and 'consolidating'.[14]

In her book *Saving the Media*, the French academic Julia Cagé gives the example of the *Chicago Tribune*. After being turned into a public company, profits rose 23 per cent per year – even though revenue only went up 9 per cent. This was achieved by one method alone: slashing expenditure, particularly on news production. There is an almost inevitable clash, Cagé concludes, between commitment to democracy and commitment to shareholders.[15]

In the UK, the Johnston Press, a family newspaper group started in the 1840s, has been bought out by hedge funds that critics accuse of similar 'vulture capitalism': starving newsrooms of investment to squeeze them for cash and, in doing so, actually hastening their demise.[16]

Hedge funds and financial institutions are an easy target. And some of their critics seem blind to the fact that almost all media owners are, at present, cutting costs and downsizing their operations. In some ways, it doesn't matter who owns a newspaper: the pressure to cut is overwhelming, given the deepening downward spiral of print revenues.

But in other ways, who owns a news outlet does matter – it matters enormously. There is a meaningful difference between a group that is specifically focused on short-term profit and one that is weathering the storm and trying to find a long-term, viable business model.[17] Ken Doctor, a media analyst for the website Newsonomics, describes the venture capitalists who own failing news outlets: 'They're not reinvesting in the business .... It's dying and they are going to make every dollar they can on the way down.'[18]

A purely commercial venture needs to focus on profits of all the parts of their operations. By contrast, a for-profit news organisation run for partly personal, philanthropic or even political reasons might be willing to accept losses in some parts of their organisation – either because they are operating on a longer-term timeframe, or because they are willing for another part of the company to cross-subsidise the loss maker.

We have seen these profit-driven 'efficiency savings' in New Zealand with widespread cuts in staffing numbers and resources. The most affected are local, rural and community newspapers. In February 2018, Stuff announced that it had identified twenty-eight newspapers it planned to close down or sell. By September 2018, twenty of these were closed. Sinead Boucher, the CEO of Stuff, described the rationale:

The business has to sustain its earnings and if there are parts that aren't doing their bit we have to make the decision to rationalise them. … We will make decisions on a publication-by-publication basis about whether they are adding value to the business or not.[19]

One senior journalist I talked to described the cuts at a newspaper that remained: 'They've essentially taken the guts out of that organisation and supplemented it with content from all directions, all in the name of cost efficiencies.'[20] Journalists were let go, and the local news they had produced in the past was replaced with copy from the national Stuff website – resulting in a product that struggled to serve the local community.

Chris Barton describes similar cuts while he was at the *New Zealand Herald* (NZME):

Redundancies became an unstoppable trend. Every few years there would be another bunch gone as the bean counters invented new ways – outsourcing sub-editing in 2007, changing to tabloid format in 2012 – to cut costs.... Beside the body count, there has also been significant collateral damage to journalism – a slow suffocation that makes it difficult for a certain type of journalism to breathe.[21]

It's important to acknowledge that Stuff and NZME are also producing a great deal of high-quality journalism. For example, Stuff has recently joined with leading organisations around the world to produce compelling climate change reporting. NZME has also produced excellent longreads, analyses and investigations, which it hopes will attract readers to subscribe online. This discussion is not a criticism of them as companies, or an attempt to draw negative generalisations across their journalistic output. Rather, its goal is to underline the financial challenges facing commercial news outlets, and the extent to which the future of journalism rests in the hands of just two companies.

The concentration of the media in New Zealand was widely discussed in 2016 when NZME and Fairfax applied to merge, and were subsequently rejected by the Commerce Commission. The Commission's final decision noted that the merger would result in an unbearably concentrated ownership of media – with almost 90 per cent of professional print and online journalism in the hands of just one media company.[22]

Supporters of the merger argued that, without it, the companies' respective news outlets would not be able to afford to produce quality journalism going forward. Thus, journalism as a whole would be poorer. Indeed, a group of editors from the two companies wrote that 'the rapid dismantling of local newsrooms and journalism at scale in this country is inevitable if this merger does not proceed'.[23] There may have been an element of fear mongering here. But the truth is that revenue is declining and there are no immediate solutions on the horizon.[24]

PUBLIC FUNDING

The fourth and final reason why New Zealand journalism is particularly vulnerable to the current crisis is that we have very little publicly funded media to fall back on. Most developed countries have determined that it is too risky to leave journalism entirely to economic forces, because the market routinely fails to produce the news we need in a healthy democracy. Emily Bell, founding director of the Tow Center for Digital Journalism at Columbia University, argues that this is even more important today, given the wider crises facing the media: 'At the moment, I think public service media has got the most important role to play that

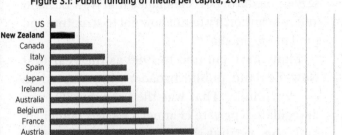

Figure 3.1: Public funding of media per capita, 2014[25]

Per capita media funding (CAD)

it's had at any point since the end of the second World War.'[26]

Most governments heavily invest in media that is free to serve the public interest. New Zealand is not among these countries. We have historically been at the bottom of every league table of developed countries, with the exception of the US. Historically, Australia has spent approximately three times as much per person, and the UK more than six times as much. New Zealand is almost alone in the industrialised Commonwealth as having no general public service TV.

Moreover, the money that is spent on public media has been poorly targeted and managed. Indeed, a prominent international report of public service media in 2011 concluded that New Zealand 'offers a cautionary tale of how not to structure and fund public media'.[27]

Many have pointed to 1989 as the year that New Zealand public broadcasting started to go 'downhill'.[28] That was the year that TV was deregulated, private channel TV3 was launched, and the ratings battle began. TVNZ was transformed from a state-owned organisation into a state-owned enterprise, and instructed that it had to turn a profit – unlike in the UK, Canada or Australia, where public media is run as not-for-profit. This resulted in the unusual situation whereby New Zealand had a public TV channel that was virtually indistinguishable from its privately owned competitors.[29]

As it turned out, TVNZ was very good at making money. Between 1989 and 1999 it sent Treasury more than $200 million.[30] But as researchers have meticulously documented, this was achieved with a sharp increase in populist content and infotainment. News items got shorter, there was a decrease in stories about politics and 'serious topics', and those that remained contained less analysis. In 1985, an interview within a news item would last an average of 18 seconds; by 1995, this had halved to 8.9 seconds – more like a soundbite.[31]

In 2003, attempting to create more public service broadcasting, the Labour Government introduced a charter that set out a number of obligations for TVNZ. These mirrored the BBC's values to 'inform, entertain and educate'. Content was also required to foster a sense of citizenship, include a significant Māori voice, extend the range of ideas available to New Zealanders, support the local TV industry, and more. These were all laudable goals. But TVNZ was not allocated resources to achieve them. The government gave TVNZ $16 million to support charter programming (the broadcaster estimated that it would cost $20–$50 million), but it was told it must also return a profit to the government. Victoria University of Wellington's Peter Thompson, the Chair of Better Public Media (a trust that aims to improve broadcasting and media in New Zealand), described this as an absurd situation in which the government was '[g]iving with one hand, and taking with the other'.[32] Between 2003 and 2008, $95 million was devoted to the charter but a much bigger $142 million was paid out in dividends – in other words, the government's net contribution was negative.

This 'dual remit' – to serve the public and also make money – was a failure. Funding was too limited and constrained by commercial objectives.[33] There were a few tweaks to programming, some token local broadcasting, but, for the most part, the commercial, ratings-driven content remained.[34] Broadcaster Mark Sainsbury gives a remarkable example of the commercial values that dominated at the time: 'I can remember one head of news and current affairs saying to us "For God's sake don't do stories about Aids – they don't rate."'[35] TVNZ's chief executive at the time, Ian Fraser, argued that the commercial pressures were 'profoundly incompatible with any recognisable model of public broadcasting'.[36] During the 2008 election campaign, TV One, supposedly driven by these charter obligations to inform and educate New Zealanders, provided almost identical news content to the commercial TV3 – in terms of the quantity, focus, depth and analysis within stories.

From 2008 to 2012, New Zealand experimented with low-budget public service channels in the form of TVNZ6 and TVNZ7. These provided news and information, but had a tiny budget by international standards, and were limited in what they could do. Introduced under Labour in recognition of the charter's failures, the channels were cut by the next National Government, which cited low viewership figures – a claim that was subsequently contested.[37] In 2011, John Key scrapped the charter completely, and TVNZ doubled down on its commercial focus.

The government's major support of TV broadcasting now comes via NZ On Air, which oversees a contestable pot of money. Approximately $40 million is tagged for factual programming. In 2016,

NZ On Air decided for the first time that digital and non-traditional broadcasters could apply for their contested fund. This was an important step to supporting digital journalism, and it has already supported quality programmes. In 2017, Stuff published 'The Valley', an impressive, multimedia investigation into New Zealand's involvement in Afghanistan, supported by a NZ On Air grant of $324,000. And the *New Zealand Herald* made 'Under the Bridge', its first full-length documentary, with $70,000 of NZ On Air funding.[38]

But public funding is still low, and commercial pressures continue to shape the journalism on our most viewed TV channels and other news outlets.

DESERTS AND OASES

What do all these financial cuts mean for the content of the news itself? In some quarters, journalism appears to be on life support: outlets are closing, and news is getting fluffier. But, confusingly, we are also living through a golden age.

Analysing this landscape, Cagé comments that '[t]here have never been as many information producers as there are today. Paradoxically, the media have never been in worse shape.'[39] Cagé and many others have described our era as a paradox but, in fact, the two observations are directly related. The internet has untethered audiences and advertisers from the traditional media. Struggling to survive, the legacy media are now experimenting with their news products. And their different strategic responses to this challenge explain the paradoxes we see. Some outlets are seeking page views above all else (the 'bikinis, sharks and crime' model). Others are investing in high-quality content in the hope this will translate into subscribers, members, brand loyalty, and more lucrative advertising opportunities or sponsorship. Some are trying multiple strategies at once.

To understand what this all means – and the areas of journalism we should worry about – we need to return to the three roles that journalism performs in a democracy, as outlined in the previous chapter. First, we rely on journalism to provide trustworthy information about the important issues of the day. Second, we rely on it to hold powerful people to account. And third, we rely on it to provide a space for us, as citizens, to debate the important issues of the day and amplify our concerns to political elites.

The following sections take each of these jobs in turn, and ask how journalism in New Zealand is performing.

INFORMATION ABOUT THE IMPORTANT ISSUES OF THE DAY

We rely on the media to provide trustworthy infor- mation about the pressing issues of the day. Over the last two decades in New Zealand, there has been a sharp drop in journalism about social and political issues – what is sometimes called 'hard news'. At the same time, there has been a rise in news about celebrities, sport, human interest, crime and the 'weird and wonderful'. This was particularly visible online in the early days of web journalism, when editors tried to publish stories that would attract large audiences and make money from digital advertising (a strategy that has not proven profitable). But it has happened across all of the major media.[40]

The *New Zealand Listener* – our most popular current affairs magazine – provides a telling example of how commercial pressures have led to an increase in lighter news content. The National Library in Wellington keeps full copies of the magazine, and I sat down and systematically read through its back issues looking at the subject matter in the cover stories of every issue from 1996 and 2016, to see how the focus had changed.

I found that, over that twenty-year period, the *Listener* had effectively repositioned itself as a lifestyle magazine. In the year 1996, two cover stories were about self-improvement: one about dieting and one about saving for retirement. By 2016, twenty-four covers – almost half of all the magazines published that year – had cover stories about self-improvement. They offered advice on how to stay slim, reduce stress, avoid dangerous microbes and survive your next surgery. Others promised to help increase happiness, improve mental agility, ward off loneliness and build wealth.

In 1996, there were eighteen cover stories that focused on policy and political issues. Some of these were about the election that was taking place that year, but many more were about broader issues such as policing, child poverty, the mismanagement of Tranz Rail, and education policy. Twenty years later, in 2016, these cover stories had practically disappeared. There were only six covers about political issues, and four of these were about international politics – primarily the US election. This left only two cover stories specifically about policy and political issues in New Zealand: one on the economics of farming, and one about the environment.

This discussion is not intended to single out the *Listener* for particular criticism. There is nothing wrong with a magazine choosing to focus on lifestyle issues, or using this content to draw in readers. As noted earlier, 'soft news' is not inherently bad. Moreover, the magazine does still contain important, well-researched journalism and analysis. But New Zealand's media market is small, and the shift in just one publication's approach has ripple effects on the state of public debate.

The most notable decline in hard news reporting has been on TV. Joe Atkinson, Honorary Research Fellow at Auckland University, has

Table 3.1: Cover stories of the *New Zealand Listener* by topic, 1996 and 2016

Topic	1996	2016	Change
Self-improvement	4%	46%	+42%
Politics and policy	35%	12%	-23%
Culture and reviews	13%	6%	-7%
Society and trends	10%	15%	+5%
Other	39%	21%	-18%

shown that there was a major 'depoliticization' of the evening TV news through the 1980s and 1990s, as broadcasters sought to maximise their ratings and circulation.[41] Sarah Baker, Lecturer at the AUT School of Communications, has meticulously compared current affairs TV shows from 1984, 1994 and 2004. Her research documents a huge jump in stories about celebrities, human interest, crime and sports personalities. One remarkable example was the current affairs show *Sunday*: in 1984, 94 per cent of this show was taken up by 'serious issues'; in 2004, this figure was only 16 per cent. The average story length fell from 23 minutes to 13 minutes, and the number of items about politics fell from 72 per cent to 7 per cent. Baker concludes: 'The decline in serious subject matter was so dramatic that some areas in effect became extinct.'[42]

For commercial companies, quality local journalism simply doesn't make financial sense. TV channels know they won't recoup the high production costs through advertising.[43] It is much cheaper to import foreign content, or to make reality TV, which has low overheads and can be extremely popular. Moreover, a relatively big audience may not be enough to keep a 'serious programme' on the air: not when an alternative programme might do better. TV host Nadine Higgins describes seeing this while working at TVNZ:

I watched show after show get cancelled or restructured – not because they didn't believe in the product or wanted to send good people packing, but because of one simple fact: they must schedule the shows that deliver the largest possible audience, for the lowest possible cost, in order to make a profit.[44]

Controversially, in 2015, MediaWorks cut *Campbell Live*, the award-winning current affairs show, as well as *3D*, its only long-form investigative programme. The latter cancellation made thirteen staff redundant, among them some of New Zealand's most experienced investigative journalists.

Amongst these cuts and downsizing, there are two areas of journalism in New Zealand that are affected the most: reporting on the regions, and reporting on the globe.

Regional and community news

Around the world, local and regional journalism has been hardest hit by the economic crisis, and New Zealand is no exception.[45] As Karin Wahl-Jorgensen, Professor at Cardiff University, writes:

[C]enters of power in nation states ... tend to be well served by news organizations [but] poorer and less densely populated areas suffer from chronic news drought. While the closure or abandonment of major urban newspapers tends to receive significant attention, the hidden big story is the growing trend of cuts, consolidation, and closure of local titles.[46]

With small populations, it is harder to make money. Making it harder still, local outlets are generally more reliant on income from classified and display adverts than national outlets.[47] There are many free local papers, for example, that rely 100 per cent on advertising revenue.

In the UK, media monitors estimate that upwards of 240 local newspapers were shut down between 2004 and 2011. As a result, some areas of the UK are no longer covered by professional journalists at all. Over half of the UK's parliamentary constituencies, 330 out of 650, are not covered by a daily local newspaper.[48]

Even in giant metropolitan centres, like London and New York, news outlets tend to chase national (or global) audiences, rather than focusing on city-based issues.[49] Paul Moses, a former City Hall journalist in New York, notes that there is almost no coverage of politics or the courts in the city's boroughs. For example:

Were it a city, New York's Queens County would be the nation's fourth largest. Police record some 35,000 major crimes a year and the local courthouse calendars upward of 200,000 criminal cases annually. But for all that activity, the courthouse press-room is locked and unoccupied: There is no reporter based in the courts of a county with more than 2.3 million residents.[50]

Similarly in New Zealand, regional newspapers have been very hard hit by closures and job cuts. The Newspaper Publishers' Association estimates that reporter numbers in regional newsrooms have fallen by at least 152 (28 per cent) in the last three to five years.[51] As previously mentioned, in 2018, Stuff, which owns the biggest group of newspapers around the country, announced that twenty-eight communication and regional newspapers would be sold or closed.[52] Surveying this media landscape in 2017, journalist Tess McClure concluded that 'if nothing changes, New Zealand faces an impending apocalypse for local public interest journalism'.[53]

Many local councils around the country are no longer reported on or scrutinised. The *Mediawatch* team at Radio New Zealand recently illustrated this through an analysis of reporting on Hutt City Council and local issues – comparing two weeks of news in November 1998 with two weeks in 2018:

A rough count revealed that the *Dominion, Evening Post* and *Hutt News* combined published 20 local body stories over the two week period in 1998 compared to none during the first two weeks of last month on the Stuff website and the Stuff-owned *Hutt News*.[54]

Simon Edwards, a Hutt City councillor, told *Mediawatch* that he hadn't seen a reporter at a council meeting for at least six months.

Ian Telfer reported on Otago and Southland for Radio New Zealand between 2011 and 2018, and he noticed these changes.[55] When he started, he would routinely see ten or so journalists at big events and press conferences; these journalists were from a range of outlets, including local newspapers, radio stations, and national and regional TV. Six years later there were half that number. The remaining journalists are also being asked to do more with their time: to cover larger geographic areas; take photos and videos; produce and edit their work; and write additional copy for websites and social media.

In many ways, Dunedin, where Telfer worked, is 'lucky': the *Otago Daily Times* (*ODT*), owned by the Allied Press, is one of a very small number of independent metropolitan newspapers in New Zealand. Although the paper is a business, it is not obliged to deliver short-term profits to any international investors. Despite the paper's falling circulation, staff numbers have remained relatively constant through the last decade. The paper is focusing on the long-term horizon, and considering a range of money-making strategies.

Historically, the *ODT* was the subject of gentle parody, particularly from students in Dunedin. Its pages are often packed with feel-good articles about high school achievers and fishing trips. But alongside these human (and animal) stories, the *ODT* serves a vital role. It is what is sometimes referred to as a 'paper of record', meaning that it documents the important issues and events regarding the governance of Otago, including council meetings, courts and resource consent issues.

Moreover, its letters, columns and, increasingly, its website and social media pages provide an important space for public debate on issues that affect the region. Should a multi-storey hotel in the Octagon get planning consent? How can we rebuild the hospital? Can the city support a professional theatre? Notably, a huge portion of the city are engaged with this public sphere – when an item appears in the newspaper's pages, people know about it.[56] With audiences around the world increasingly fragmented, and exposed to different media content, this is a rare trait. It brings people into conversation about their political community.

Local news also plays a very important, but often invisible, role supporting the national news. At its best, national reporting covers important events and issues from around the country. It explores how issues like minimum wage, water pollution and immigration are affecting different communities – and not just the large urban centres. And it also pieces these events together to identify trends – it might spot, for example, that the rates of drowning are on the rise, or that shops on the main street are struggling.

To do this work effectively, national media needs local inputs – information coming from around the regions. Rasmus Nielsen, Professor of Political Communication at Oxford University, describes local news outlets as 'keystone media' – borrowing a term from ecology. In the natural world, keystone species are those that play a particularly important role in the ecosystem, because other species – and therefore the wider system – rely on them.[57] In the same way, keystone media have systemic importance for the wider information environment.

Nielsen illustrates this with a detailed case study of the informational landscape of a region in Denmark. Surveys showed that only 30 per cent of citizens thought the local paper was 'important' or 'very important' to their news habits. But when the information flows were analysed, it became clear that these local outlets were at the centre of news production. They provided more than 65 per cent of the information about local issues and, significantly, this content was crucial for numerous other outlets that the audiences *did* think were important.

In Dunedin, Telfer explains that it became harder for him to do national reporting, as local publications around the South Island have shrunk:

The real damage has been the loss of strong, local newspapers going to all the court appearances and councils and documenting them like a paper of record. That is a big loss for us. Because as a national news organisation we just can't be at all that stuff – we never were, and we never can be. ... I feel like the system is breaking down. The local feeders are just so stretched and under-resourced that they're not able to do good, solid, reliable coverage. ... So that means it's not filtering up to the national media, and that means the national media is more fickle, only offering partial information. ... there's a whole lot of things that don't get covered.[58]

One of the biggest blows to regional reporting in New Zealand was the closure of the New Zealand Press Association (NZPA) in 2011, which shut after more than 130 years of sharing news around the county. National news agencies have historically played a crucial role in providing verified, fact-based news to media organisations in most countries. They are widely seen as the backbone of information flows, collating the news from around the country. New Zealand is almost alone in the developed world (and much of the developing world) in not having a national newswire.

Almost all the newspapers in New Zealand were members of NZPA. They supplied their hometown journalism to the wire, who sub-edited it in Wellington and then redistributed it to media around the country who could reprint it. This shared content was complemented with original content written by approximately forty NZPA journalists, primarily based in the parliamentary Press Gallery. In total, the wire shared up to 1,000 daily news items.[59]

In 2006, NZPA adopted a more commercial model. It stopped sharing member content in a collaborative system, and started to sell its journalism. In 2011, Fairfax pulled out of the agreement, believing they could do the same thing for their outlets more cheaply. NZPA could not function without the subscription money from Fairfax, and it shut down.

Former editor of the *New Zealand Herald* Gavin Ellis, who has written a book about NZPA,[60] describes the impact of its closure on journalism as:

[A]n unmitigated disaster. One of the most short-sighted moves ... this idiotic attitude of competition really became a be all and end all. ... You'll hear people say NZPA had outlived its usefulness: bullshit. They both thought: we can do this cheaper and better ourselves. Both set up their equivalent service, neither of which equalled NZPA at all and still cost money.[61]

There have been recent, welcome moves among New Zealand outlets to share some journalistic content. In 2018, Radio New Zealand had content-sharing arrangements with twenty-five organisations, and was planning more;[62] Stuff has arrangements with Bauer Media, TVNZ and *Newsroom*. This is helping to share resources and extend the reach of news stories. But it is not yet systematic or nationwide.

The neglect of the globe

In addition to a shortage of local news, the New Zealand news media contains shockingly low levels of international news. One study of print, TV and radio content found that only 2.6 per cent of news items could be considered 'global' in focus.[63] And a huge portion of this tiny amount of international news focused on just three countries: Australia, the US and the UK. Canterbury University media researcher Donald Matheson found that these three countries accounted for 43 per cent of international news. Moreover, Matheson found that almost all international news published in New Zealand is second-hand, taken from global news agencies such as Reuters and AFP, rather than reported with a New Zealand audience in mind. In total, 95 per cent of all our international news content comes directly from the international newswires.[64]

These figures are deeply troubling. New Zealand is directly involved in or affected by countless global issues and events – a fact that was shockingly underlined by the Christchurch terror attacks. The most important and pressing social and political issues of our time are transnational: climate change, trade agreements, military alliances, data management and intelligence alliances, to name a few. Our government has policies on these issues, which need to be discussed and debated alongside news coverage of the events themselves.

In my final year at Otago University, I wrote a dissertation on news coverage of New Zealand's decision to support conflict in Afghanistan. I spent hours trawling through the country's newspapers, counting the sources who spoke and the topics they discussed. The results were disturbing. The decision to send SAS soldiers to Afghanistan – which would become one of New Zealand's most intractable conflicts – was barely debated. Domestically, news stories focused on the political 'game playing', and rarely analysed the claims politicians were making: the ethics, logistics or ramifications of invasion. Meanwhile, there was plenty of coverage about the US-led invasion of Afghanistan, but this rarely ever mentioned New Zealand, because it was content taken from newswires. This resulted in a disconnect between what was happening 'out there' and our direct role in the conflict.

A lack of knowledge about the world can be a very dangerous thing. Researchers have demonstrated that levels of knowledge (and ignorance) about international events have a direct bearing on foreign policy preferences.[65] In one disarming study, researchers surveyed more than 2,000 Americans and asked them how the US should respond to Russia's annexing of Crimea from Ukraine. They found that the less the respondents knew about the location of Ukraine, the more likely they were to want to intervene with military force.[66]

Even where international news stories do not have a direct and obvious link to New Zealand, it is helpful for reports to be tailored to a New Zealand audience. Such stories can highlight why an event is interesting or important, and draw connections for the audience about the place of New Zealand in the globe – for example, identifying connections between the crisis in Syria and the support of refugees from that region in New Zealand, or noting connections and flow in terms of trade, cultural exchange and so on. Even small modifications to newswire stories can make stories more accessible.

To give a small example, when news outlets in Europe reported on the conflict in the Darfur region of Sudan, they would refer to Darfur as an area 'roughly the size of France'. In the US, they described it as 'roughly the size of Texas'. Researchers have shown that when stories are 'domesticised' in this way, audiences are more likely to engage and understand the content.[67]

It is not surprising that original international news coverage has shrunk in New Zealand. Foreign bureaux were among the first casualties of journalism's economic downturn in the early 2000s. In just six years, between 2000 and 2006, there was a 10–30 per cent decline in the number of US newspaper-sponsored foreign bureaux. TV networks have also been extensively cut; there are no US network bureaux left in Africa, India or South America, regions that are home to more than 2 billion people.[68] Original international news content is now a luxury that very few news organisations can afford.

I recently completed a study of international reporting with some colleagues in the UK. We searched the news outputs of more than 20,000 English-language news outlets to discover how they reported on four important humanitarian issues in 2016. Quite shockingly, we found that only twelve of the news outlets reported on all four of these issues.[69]

It is too much to expect that the New Zealand media would be able to produce comprehensive original reporting on the world, given the economic pressures it is under. But we could hope to see, at a minimum, some consistent, original reporting about countries in the Pacific, with which we share direct and important cultural, political and environmental ties. Too often Pacific islands are grouped together as a homogenous unit, and only reported on when there is crisis or disaster.[70] It would be good to see governments in the Pacific giving journalists greater access to do this reporting, as well.[71] Moreover, we would ideally have more time and resources to 'domesticate' global stories taken from newswires, and help explain their importance to a New Zealand audience.

CRITICAL REPORTING

The second key job that journalism performs in a democracy is holding those with power to account. This is the media's classic role as the 'watchdog of the powerful', which is done through both investigative journalism and daily monitoring and reporting. This section considers how the New Zealand media is performing against these criteria. We see that there are shortages of resources for this work, and even more concerningly, perhaps, that those with power have very sophisticated, image-crafting marketing teams that are often better resourced than the journalists reporting on them.

Investigative journalism

New Zealand investigative journalists, given time and resources, are among the best in the world.

Two of the biggest media groups – NZME and Stuff – both have small, experienced teams that have investigated topics from MPs meddling in police matters to the treatment of disabled children and the financial investments of KiwiSaver. This journalism has led to political resignations and policy change. There are also a number of newer outlets, like *Newsroom*, making a big impact. But this critical investigative journalism is also constantly under-resourced, and often done on an ad hoc basis. As a result, there is limited routine scrutiny of those with power.

One of the quirks of our small media system is that a lot of important investigative journalism is done outside the mainstream media, by 'lone wolves' rather than the proverbial 'watchdogs'. It is much harder for journalists to do investigative reporting alone. This is partly for financial reasons. Many investigations are incredibly slow, requiring weeks, months and even years to piece together information and pursue leads. Harold Evans, for example, the legendary editor of *The Times* (UK), spent more than a decade doggedly seeking justice for the victims of the thalidomide scandal. And while Evans' campaign has had positive outcomes, many such investigations may lead to dead ends, with years of sunk costs and wasted research.

Lone journalists do not have professional support, either. Alan Rusbridger, who oversaw numerous investigations while editor of the *Guardian*, describes the challenge:

If their reporting genuinely challenges power, they will need organisational courage behind them. They will need sharp-eyed text editors and ingenious lawyers. They may require people with sophisticated technological or security know-how. If they get into trouble they may need immediate logistical, medical, legal, financial or PR back-up.[72]

Rusbridger details a range of investigations during his time as editor that would not have been possible without the support of a very well-resourced newsroom. These include revelations of corrupt MPs, fraudulent arms deals, a fake vitamin scam, the publication of the Wikileaks documents, and the Edward Snowden leaks. In many of these investigations, the organisation was directly threated by lawyers, the police and Parliament: 'A single journalist on their own could be picked off and silenced. A journalist doing brave work needed to know their organisation would defend their reporting.'[73]

Greenslade echoes this sentiment, arguing that '[b]ig government and big business needs big media to hold them to account: the sniper will never be as successful as the tank and the cannon.'[74]

New Zealand's best-known 'lone wolf' is Nicky Hager. Working alone, Hager does not enjoy the financial support or legal protection of an established media outlet. In 2014, his house was illegally raided by the police in an attempt to uncover his sources.

Working alone, Hager is also more vulnerable to accusations of bias. In 2016, after he shared the findings of the Panama Papers that highlighted New Zealand's role as an international tax haven, Prime Minister John Key called him a 'left-wing conspiracy theorist'.[75] Hager's conclusions had come from the leaked documents of the firm Mossack Fonseca. But it was not until other media outlets joined the call for an investigation that Key launched a review, and ultimately changed the tax laws.[76] Hager is a polarising journalist, but this treatment should set off alarm bells. He is a leading investigative journalist, and for some time was New Zealand's only representative on the International Consortium of Investigative Journalists, the major world body that coordinates international investigations like the Panama Papers.

The most profound gap for investigative journalism in New Zealand, however, is on TV, where there is essentially no regular investigative programme. This is notable because TV remains one of the most popular sources of news, and is a powerful forum in which to raise awareness of injustice. While she was working at *3D*, Paula Penfold's team investigated the wrongful murder conviction of Teina Pora, and helped to secure his release. Tim McKinnel, a detective who worked on the case, looked back on the acquittal and commented:

It is hard to overstate the vital role their investigative journalism played in advancing Teina's case. Witnesses came forward and spoke to the appeal team and to police as a result of their work and new evidence emerged and was developed by both sides of the appeal.[77]

Print journalists had been writing about Pora's case, but it wasn't until it appeared on *3D* that the story began to develop real momentum in the public eye. That's the 'power of television', Penfold told journalist Adam Dudding: 'There's something in that immediacy and in that palpable physicality in seeing that person and hearing their words.'[78]

Having seen the potential of this journalism, McKinnel was furious when MediaWorks decided to cut the show:

I watch with desperation as the MediaWorks team proposes cancelling their last investigative journalism program. ... I suspect Mr Weldon [CEO of MediaWorks at the time] will tell us ... *3D* was expensive, out of date, not snackable, ratings were low (not surprisingly given the constant shifting of its timeslot), and that the program did not provide the value MediaWorks' owners require. That's all bullshit. The value of *3D*, of any investigative journalism, can't be measured by ratings. In Teina's case, those journalists were the critical difference between New Zealanders understanding justice and injustice.[79]

The power of images in investigative journalism was again illustrated in 2019 when *Newsroom* published Melanie Reid's important investigation into child 'uplifting' by Oranga Tamariki. The documentary footage follows one teenager's fight to keep her baby, and the consistent pressure she faced from child services.[80] Reid and others had previously written on this topic – specifically noting the rates at which Oranga Tamariki 'uplifted' babies from Māori and Pasifika families. But it was not until the publication of the video that the story gained traction – when audiences could see with their own eyes the young mother asked over and over again to hand over her baby. As *Mediawatch*'s Colin Peacock writes: 'Perhaps the startling scenes in *Newsroom*'s video this week show New Zealanders still have to see it to believe it.'[81] This reporting also demonstrated that video does not need to be broadcast on TV to have a wide reach and impact: multimedia packages on websites, backed by credible news brands, can be just as effective.

The contribution of quality, critical multimedia journalism goes beyond the justice gains associated with a particular case. It also plays an important role in building public trust in the media. Done well, it *shows* the audience a professional journalist at work – demonstrating professionalism and the meticulous research process. This is precisely the kind of work that helps to build trust in journalism as an institution.

Public relations and spin, spin, spin

Investigative journalism is not the only way that the media operates as a 'watchdog of the powerful'. Everyday journalists report on the day-to-day operation of power, asking critical questions. In this role, it is essential that the media does not simply pass messages straight from politicians or lobbyists to the public: they also need to check facts, examine, critique and question the claims of elites.[82] A major challenge to this work are the very well-resourced politicians, consultants, businesses, charities, marketers and others who actively seek to influence the news agenda.

Journalists do not always have the time to critique this content. In his bestselling book *Flat Earth News*, Nick Davies describes the pressures on UK journalists, who are often expected to write close to ten stories a day. To achieve this near-impossible target, journalists repurpose second-hand material: press releases, social media posts and stories from other news outlets. Working with a group of academics from Cardiff University, Davies analysed 2,200 news stories in the UK and found that the vast majority – even at high-quality newspapers like the *Guardian* and *The Times* – were taken straight from newswires or press releases:

No reporter who is turning out nearly ten stories every shift can possibly do his or her job properly … build enough good contacts … [or] be checking their truth. This is churnalism. This is journalism failing to perform the simple basic functions of their profession; quite unable to tell their readers the truth about what is happening on their patch. This is journalists who are no longer out gathering news but who are reduced instead to passive processors of whatever material comes their way, churning out stories, whether real event or PR, artifice, important or trivial, true or false.[83]

This 'churnalism' – and the dominance of press release material in journalism – has become commonplace in New Zealand. Some estimate that as much as half of all the content in a newspaper or news bulletin can be traced back to media releases or other public relations activity. Helen Sissons is a leading researcher at Auckland University of Technology, where she has researched this phenomenon. In a 2016 study, Sissons traced thirty-five press releases written by companies and event organisers in New Zealand. She found that a remarkable twenty-three of them were reproduced almost word-for-word in the news.[84] The remaining twelve were published with some reworking; only two were changed substantially.

This is not surprising when we look at the

resource imbalance between journalists and marketing teams. In the 2013 Census, public relations professionals outnumbered journalists by a remarkable three to one.[85] And these public relations workers are often more senior and experienced than the average journalist. Indeed, many worked in senior journalism posts before 'jumping ship' (or 'turning to the dark side', as less charitable commentators put it).

Public relations is not inherently bad. Indeed, many marketing and publicity teams do important work communicating information to the public. Campaigns around public health are perhaps the best example: highlighting issues around drinking, smoking, wearing seat belts, applying sunscreen and so on, with the goal of improving well-being. Public relations and marketing are also an important feature of social justice campaigns.[86]

Public relations and marketing also play an important role subsidising journalism – although journalists rarely like to admit it.[87] These professionals help by doing some of the leg work required to report on an issue or event, such as collecting information and making it available to journalists in an easy-to-use package, like a press release or press conference. They might also organise events and subsidise travel and expenses that can help them report.[88]

But slick, well-resourced public relations teams

are a problem when journalists do not have the time to do their own research and fact checking. And with dwindling time and resources, journalists frequently rely on the contents of press releases for quick, inexpensive news.[89] Former MP Steve Maharey, for example, describes the ease he had influencing news content while in office:

[M]ost of the news stories about the work I do as a Labour spokesperson and MP for Palmerston North originate from my office. I literally write the news stories quoting myself which are then sent out as media releases. Quite often these releases appear relatively unchanged in the news under the byline of a staff reporter or named journalist.[90]

To a large extent, politicians can dictate the setting, timing and tone of reporting. Patrick Gower, former TV3 journalist and now National Correspondent for *Newshub*, described one such instance to Massey University media researcher Margie Comrie. For months, Gower had been ringing a government department to ask if a potentially embarrassing report about a high-level military appointment was available. Eventually the report was dumped on a Friday when there were other big stories and the political journalists were busy. The dump of potentially embarrassing material is, Gower said, 'classic Manipulation 101. You do get frustrated. In fact, it happens so much, you probably don't get frustrated enough.'[91]

Government departments and agencies also have slick media teams and communication strategies that can make it difficult for journalists to access information and frank opinions. The police have launched a 24-hour media station in Wellington, for example – journalists that want information are required to use this official team, whose job is to help maintain the image of the police force. In the past, journalists cultivated close relationships directly with local police. This is on the rise: a recent review of employees at government ministries found that the number of public sector communications staff has risen 60 per cent since 2013.[92] Again, this is not necessarily a negative development – it is in everyone's interest that the government has professional teams collating information and making it public and accessible. More and more journalist–source interaction takes place on terms that suit the officials. Pattrick Smellie, who has worked in PR and government, as well as journalism, argues that it makes it more difficult for journalists to speak to decision-makers and people at the helm of policy-making.[93]

In principle, the Official Information Act (OIA) makes it possible for journalists to obtain detailed information about government actions. But OIA requests are often dealt with very slowly, and with sensitive information (as defined by those in charge) redacted. Newstalk ZB chief political reporter Felix Marwick describes the frustration of trying to get information:

If you use the OIA to get something that doesn't cast officials or politicians or departments in the best light, they'll find reasons not to release it to you. And then your only option is to go to the Ombudsman, which can turn into a long, drawn out process by which time when you finally get a result – in this case three years – its relevance is lessened. The system can be used, by those we're trying to scrutinise, to basically impede, block, stymie, the release of information that is critical to those involved.[94]

More prosaically, officials may not have the resources – or the know-how – to comply with journalists' requests.

Ask around at any gathering of journalists and you'll hear numerous examples of obstruction, delays and unhelpful responses. Many find it one of the most frustrating aspects of writing political stories, and an area desperately in need of reform. Eugene Bingham, a producer from TV3's former current affairs show *3D*, recalls a request for information about police crime statistics that was stalled for two years.[95] Kirsty Johnston, an investigative journalist at the *New Zealand Herald*, recalls a project on water extraction where she contacted every regional and city council in New Zealand to request information about their water management. Many seemed completely unaware of their obligation to share public information, and the experience left Johnston concerned that they were very rarely scrutinised.[96] Gavin Ellis outlines some of these concerns in his book *Complacent Nation*, arguing for a major reform and overhaul of the OIA system.[97]

Private companies also spend an enormous amount of time and money trying to influence news content. They pay 'experts' to give testimony to the media, create press releases and campaigns, and orchestrate events and statements designed to look like they have come, unprompted, from ordinary citizens (a phenomenon sometimes referred to as 'astroturfing': an artificial take on the 'grassroots movement'). This was famously done by tobacco companies through the mid to late twentieth century, and it is still done today by companies whose products harm people and the environment.[98]

Nicky Hager has detailed a number of these campaigns in New Zealand, including one by a US public relations company hired to lobby for the continued logging of native forestry. According to Hager, the company invented a pro-logging campaign (including a fake pro-logging community group) and attacked the credibility of environmentalists who opposed them. During several years of political and media debate, Hager noted that almost all news organisations quoted the fake community group, without realising it was a fabrication designed to advance the strategy of the logging industry.[99]

Shaun Hendy, Professor of Physics at the University of Auckland, describes these tactics in his book *Silencing Science*:

On issues like climate change, water quality or public health, special interest groups have developed strategies to undermine the credibility of scientists. When this happens, politicians can be drawn into the fray, and the government can find itself facing off against its own scientists.[100]

Muddying the waters further, political consultants and lobbyists working for politicians and businesses are often given prominent media platforms to comment on political issues, and their affiliations and clients are not always disclosed.[101]

In addition to their lack of time, journalists often do not have the specialisation or expertise to question marketing content. Among the cuts in journalist numbers and the restructuring, newsrooms have lost a huge depth of experience. Karl du Fresne, a former newspaper editor, writes, '[w]aves of editorial redundancies, imposed to cut costs … have resulted in an enormous loss of institutional knowledge.' Casualties include the journalists with deep specialist knowledge in areas such as education, business and industrial relations. And – as many readers will have noticed – the sub-editors, whose job was to keep errors out of the paper.[102]

Science reporting is particularly challenging when journalists do not have a background in the area. Universities often invest in public relations teams to help build their reputation and celebrate their teaching and research. In this promotional material, they have been known to overstate the significance of research findings or to simplify them to catch media attention. A *British Medical Journal* study of 405 university press releases about research papers found that 40 per cent of the releases contained health advice that was more explicit than anything in the original research article. One-third of the releases suggested there was causation when the research had only found correlations, and 36 per cent over-inflated the relevance of the research to humans, when the studies had been on cells or animals.[103] A recent survey of international journalists found that 53 per cent were not confident of their ability to tell good research from bad.[104]

The net result of growing marketing budgets, and declining journalism resources, is that the media is vulnerable to being co-opted by politicians, businesses, or others with an agenda.[105]

Some are hopeful that digital platforms will lead to the flourishing of new forms of critical, public interest journalism. James Hollings, the editor of *A Moral Truth*, describes the trend:

[A]s some of the great mastheads of yore have cut or scaled back their investigative teams, a new breed of investigator has started to fill the gap. Independent, usually operating alone, publishing entirely online, and funded by donation, crowdsourcing or other jobs.[106]

One example is *New Zealand Herald* journalist Keith Ng who, while working freelance as a writer and blogger, made important contributions to government accountability. In one piece of work, Ng discovered that the Ministry of Social Development had left sensitive personal files of citizens unprotected in public kiosks. This included the names and addresses of children being protected from domestic violence or sexual abuse, as well as those of hundreds of thousands of people accessing benefits: 'This stuff was all a few clicks away at any WINZ kiosk, anywhere in the country. The privacy breach is massive, and the safety of vulnerable children was put at risk.'[107]

Independent investigators like Ng make an important contribution, but they cannot routinely scrutinise those in power, or keep an eye on the country's courts and local councils. Moreover, they may not have secure revenue streams, and it is easier for elites to ignore or undermine their investigations.

The digital start-up *Newsroom* was founded by some of the industry's most experienced journalists, including staff who left TV3 after the closure of

3D. Since its launch in 2017, *Newsroom* has had a number of impressive 'stings', uncovering scandal across political offices, law firms and chicken farms. The outlet got one of the biggest journalistic 'scalps' of 2017 with an investigation into former National MP Todd Barclay's secret recording of staff in his Gore office. This was an important, clear cut, public interest story and *Newsroom* should be celebrated for its discovery. But it is striking that this behaviour was not identified or reported by the traditional mainstream media, even though Barclay's behaviour was an 'open secret'. As Melanie Reid, the *Newsroom* journalist who uncovered the story, commented: 'Everybody knew about it … Down in the South Island they talked about it.' The reason it hadn't been reported before, Reid believed, was that it happened in the regions: 'This story wasn't in Wellington, you had to go to Gore to get the story. The real story lay with [National Party employees] and supporters in places like Queenstown, and Balclutha and the electorate.'[108] Places, it would seem, where there is simply not enough routine scrutiny of the daily exercise of power.

FORUM FOR DEBATE
The third and final role that journalists play is providing a space for us, as citizens, to debate the important issues of the day and amplify our concerns to political elites. This is another area

where commercial squeeze, and the push for readers and ratings, are having a negative impact on content – in New Zealand and around the world.

In 2005, I spent the summer as a research fellow at Auckland University analysing TV coverage of New Zealand's election campaign. As a junior researcher, I had the unenviable task of watching the election debates over and over again and breaking them down, second by second, to record who talked, for how long, and what was said. I became intimately familiar with the facial expressions and nose hairs of our leading parliamentarians. I also became disenchanted with the quality of political debate as I recorded interjections, ad hominem attacks and a failure to discuss policy, time and time again. While political debate here is not the bear pit we see in the US and elsewhere, it is far from ideal.

David Cohen, former media commentator at the *National Business Review*, suggests that little has changed since I did that analysis. Election debates today are 'basically parallel press conferences, episodic exercises in brevity and the regurgitation of market-tested lines that have little to do with sustained political discussion'.[109]

More generally, political journalism has become overwhelmingly focused on 'the game' – the political winners and losers and the competition itself – what some researchers call 'horse race reporting'.[110]

In the first question of the first election debate

of 2017, Mike Hosking asked then Prime Minister Bill English, 'Why are you losing?', referring to a poll from earlier in the day. We are so used to the focus on competition and the 'horse race' in our political coverage that this seemed like an obvious question. Yet, it had little to do with the core issues on which the election was being fought.

As scholars Joseph Cappella and Kathleen Jamieson argue in their book *Spiral of Cynicism*, this type of reporting can actively damage the public sphere because it increases cynicism.[111] Politics is depicted as a spectacle – an arena where candidates 'perform' to try and win – and not a space where they attempt to solve collective issues, or say what they think.

Moreover, as Dannagal Young at the University of Delaware argues, an excessive focus on 'the game' reduces public trust in elites and public institutions, decreases voter turnout, and makes the public think that politics is more polarised than it is:

Put simply, journalists' reliance on this practice is allowing elites to … avoid scrutiny, and distract citizens away from thoughtful policy debate on issues that carry real-life consequences.[112]

This is not the thoughtful public debate 'outside the control of the state' that Jürgen Habermas had in mind.[113] Max Rashbrooke, whose work addresses complicated questions in economics and social inequality, rightly notes that:

Many issues are complex and multi-layered, and can only be grappled with through prolonged debate, through a free and constructive exchange of views. Being good at that requires us all to be gentler: more respectful of others' opinions, less defensive of our own positions, less certain of our own absolute rightness.[114]

This form of lengthy, constructive, rational and inclusive debate may not ever be possible: but it is a goal worth striving for.

As news moved online, many commentators became concerned that 'filter bubbles' and 'echo chambers' would increase polarisation and make the level of political debate even worse. They feared audiences would only read news and opinions that confirmed their pre-existing world view, and there would be no room for consensus building or open-minded debate. Perhaps surprisingly, recent research has suggested that the idea of an 'echo chamber' is – for the majority of the population – a myth. In fact, a growing body of research shows precisely the opposite – when people consume news online, they are exposed to a wider range of ideas than they would be offline.[115] When audiences get their news through traditional offline sources, they tend to rely on just one or two outlets – a favoured newspaper, radio station or TV channel. And this *does* limit the range of views to which they are exposed (especially in countries like the UK or US, where TV channels and newspapers can be highly partisan). Online, by contrast, users might see a very wide range of sources, and stumble upon outlets they would never normally read – what some researchers have called 'automated serendipity'.[116]

Social media groupings are not as politically homogenous as some think, and therefore going onto Facebook or Twitter can result in exposure to varied content. In one Pew Research Center survey, for example, only 2 per cent of respondents stated that they 'always' or 'nearly always' saw content they agreed with on Facebook, with 21 per cent saying they 'mostly' saw content they agreed with. But the majority – 62 per cent – said that only some of the news they saw had similar views to them, and 13 per cent said they didn't often see news they agreed with at all.[117]

There are, of course, a small number of people who read news online and only visit one or two sources. But these tend to be light users of the news, and the sources they go to tend to be large, relatively centrist outlets (for example, *USA Today* or the BBC). Interestingly, users who visit more partisan sites – for example, Breitbart or HuffPost – are often heavy media consumers with a strong interest in politics. And they tend to consume more of everything, including centrist sites and occasionally sites with conflicting ideology. As some researchers comment: 'Their omnivorousness outweighs their ideological extremity, preventing their overall news diet from becoming too skewed.'[118] This varied news diet does not appear to change the views of these outliers (who, we should note, may be reading the mainstream media to 'troll' or disagree with others). But it is a reminder that we need a nuanced analysis that does not attribute 'extreme' political views to 'echo chambers' alone.

And while algorithms do try to show people more of the news they 'like', most people like news that has a range of traits – for example, it's interesting, new and different, or on a subject they care about. Partisanship is only one of many factors that feed into a search engine's predictions.[119]

One study used survey data from the UK, US, Germany and Spain to compare the news that citizens were exposed to. In all four countries, the researchers found that 'using search engines for news is associated with more diverse and more balanced news consumption', and leads people to sources they would not have used otherwise.[120]

Moreover, studies suggest that online news consumption can, in some instances, lead to lower levels of partisanship, and higher levels of political participation.[121] This is particularly the case among young people and audiences who are not interested in the news: these groups 'accidentally' read news online that they wouldn't otherwise, and this can foster political participation.[122]

Representation, diversity and trolls

In the ideal state, the news media provides a platform for public debate that lets a wide range of perspectives speak. It does not simply platform representatives of the majority or the most powerful. In some ways, the New Zealand media compares favourably with other countries in this regard. But we have several blindspots that undermine the equality and representativeness of our public sphere, including the media representation of our cultural diversity and the treatment of women.

Representation of diversity

Around the world, it is common for the news media to neglect or misrepresent minority groups. In his important book *Racism and the Press*, Teun A. van Dijk, a pioneering linguist who helped to develop the field of critical discourse analysis, analyses two decades of research on media reporting in North America and Europe. He concludes that, almost without exception, the media in these regions promotes and reinforces the supremacy of white citizens, with minority ethnic groups depicted as 'a problem or a threat, and mostly in association with crime, violence, conflict, unacceptable cultural differences, or other forms of deviance'.[123]

The late, celebrated cultural theorist Stuart Hall is another important voice in this research literature. His work showed that black people in the UK were generally depicted as less civilised, culturally inferior and a threat to the social order. One of the key reasons for this, Hall argued, is that media content is shaped by 'primary definers' – elites in society (such as politicians, business leaders and so on) that journalists turn to over and over again for their quotes and analysis. These leaders tend to come from the dominant cultural group (and may also therefore have a vested interest in the continuation of the status quo).

New Zealand media is no exception. News coverage tends to neglect and stereotype ethnic minorities. In the mainstream commercial media, there is a paucity of Māori news content, and what exists is often marginalised and negative. Māori sources and experts are absent from news stories – even when the news is directly investigating Māori issues.[124]

One 2006 study, from the research group Kupu Taea, examined a twenty-one-day sample of TV news across multiple channels, which included 123 bulletins and 2,100 news items. The researchers found that on the English-language news shows only 1.59 per cent of news items featured Māori. Of these, an unbelievable 57 per cent were about child abuse.[125] These were not the only important events and issues of the day affecting Māori. The authors examined the content of the Māori-language news and found a far greater diversity of topics and items, which were also 'newsworthy' by industry standards.

This finding has been confirmed by one study after another.[126] Indeed, as media academic Thomas Owen comments, '[t]he negative representation of Māori in mainstream news is perhaps the most rigorously tested and consistently demonstrated finding in New Zealand media research'.[127]

Māori journalists have also described marginalisation of their programmes and content. Early in her career, Mihingarangi Forbes worked for *Te Karere*, a Māori news programme, where she recalls having poor equipment and support: 'We battled for camera crews and editors on a daily basis, only to be handed the trainees or, to be frank, the crews no one else wanted to work with.'[128] It was not uncommon for their news stories to be cancelled when, for example, the tennis ran too long. Finally leaving the programme, Forbes commented: 'I was just sick of being treated as the last cab off the rank.'[129]

Reporting on Pasifika issues and people in the New Zealand media is also dominated by negative frames and white perspectives. As Tapu Misa writes:

Like Māori, Pasifika weren't visible in any good way. We were overstayers, violent criminals and bludgers. Poor, sick, pathetic, hopeless people who couldn't cope outside our small islands …

we're still a long way from a nuanced portrayal of Māori and Pasifika communities in the media.[130]

One study of sixty-five print news reports found that Pasifika people are predominantly portrayed as unmotivated, unhealthy and criminal 'others' who are overly dependent on Palagi support.[131] In total, 92 per cent of the news reports portrayed Pasifika people in negative terms. And they were overwhelmingly framed as 'others' to the Pākehā majority's 'us'. The study also found that Pasifika people were rarely cited as sources within the news – even in stories specifically about Pacific issues.

A major contributing factor to these stereotypical representations may be the lack of diversity within New Zealand newsrooms. Of the general population, 15 per cent are Māori, but they only represent 7.9 per cent of journalists. Meanwhile, Pasifika journalists make up a tiny 1.8 per cent of journalists – compared with about 7 per cent of the total New Zealand population.[132] The lack of cultural diversity in the media is not unique to New Zealand. In the UK, for example, Black Britons make up approximately 3 per cent of the population, but just 0.2 per cent of journalists. And Asian Britons, who represent approximately 7 per cent of the UK population, make up only 2.5 per cent of journalists.[133] But that does not make it a less significant issue for New Zealand.

Diversity on university journalism courses in New Zealand is also very low. Tara Ross, Head of Journalism at the University of Canterbury, believes that it is hard to attract minority students into journalism when they do not see themselves represented in the media: '[T]here is no appetite for wanting to be part of an industry that is often seen by minorities as being racist.'[134]

This under-representation likely contributes to the fact that much journalism in New Zealand is reported through a 'white gaze'. The default assumption is that the audience of the news is Pākehā, and other world views are deviations from this 'norm'.[135] As Ray Nairn and colleagues write: 'Although Pākehā are rarely named as a group, they are constructed as natural, the nation, the ordinary, the community, against which all other ethnic groupings are viewed and measured.'[136]

One small but telling example is that the ethnicity of a news subject is rarely mentioned unless they are non-white. Michalia Arathimos, a writer and academic, documented this phenomenon in newspaper reporting of famous New Zealand authors. She found that the Māori, Tongan and Eastern European authors in her study were described in terms of their ethnicity almost every time they were mentioned, while white New Zealanders and white English writers were not. Arathimos concluded that: 'The "we" who authorizes, who polices, who celebrates or who forgets, ultimately maintains their position as the manager of the national space. And that manager, if we dissect their cultural identity, is white.'[137]

This is perhaps at its most obvious – and significant – when it comes to journalism about the Treaty claim process. Through the 1970s, 80s and 90s, in particular, and still sometimes today, claims by iwi are represented in mainstream journalism as Māori demands that would take something from 'us'.[138] In one study from 2007, researchers found that most stories about the Treaty of Waitangi were written from a Pākehā perspective and represented Māori as a source of problems or conflict in the process. The team also identified, and criticised, the widespread use of a 'Māori privilege' frame.[139]

Aaron Smale has also articulately described the default 'whiteness' of newsrooms in New Zealand, and the challenges of navigating this as a Māori journalist:

The education system has failed to educate children in New Zealand's history. The media has perpetuated and amplified that failure by not informing the adult public about people who are not white ... in many cases it has actively used its power to create and maintain a negative attitude towards people who are not white, whether they be Māori or other ethnic groups. There's an inability to interrogate white racism because there's an inability to understand what it's like to be subjected to it.[140]

Public media outlets have, in some ways, done a much better job of including diverse views. Māori Television, in particular, has been described as a world leader in indigenous broadcasting, and it has become a popular feature of the New Zealand media landscape, with approximately 1.8 million viewers per month.[141] This has been attributed to the channel's approach of melding education and entertainment content. The station is not without controversy, however. In the late 2000s, in particular, many raised concerns about the management style and the marginalisation of news journalism at the channel, which led to a series of very senior journalists departing.[142]

Nonetheless, the channel's core goal is the development and protection of the Māori language, and evaluations suggest it is having success in this area.[143] In one assessment, Jessica Beaux Ormsby Paul surveyed and conducted focus groups with audience members, and found that Māori Television had an 'overwhelmingly positive effect on the lives of its Māori viewers'. It increased accessibility, inclusion, connectedness, a sense of identity and autonomy in te ao Māori.[144]

The channel has also achieved a strong viewership beyond the Māori community. Jo Smith and Sue Abel argue that this is partly because there is no real public service TV outside Māori Television.[145] Programmes that might, in another country, be on the general PSB channel – for example, broadcasts of live ceremonies and documentaries marking ANZAC Day – are taking place on Māori Television. Five years after it was launched, most New Zealanders surveyed (84 per cent) believed that Māori Television should be a permanent fixture of New Zealand broadcasting. Many Māori (73 per cent), and about half of all New Zealanders (46 per cent), also believed that Māori Television made a valuable contribution to New Zealand's sense of nationhood.[146]

Radio New Zealand has also done some positive work in supporting media diversity, including appointing Pasifika and Māori journalists to important editorial and executive positions, and leading in the use of te reo Māori during mainstream broadcasting.[147] However, many suggest it has not gone far enough, and that there is often limited diversity among the flagship presenters.[148]

Islamophobia
After the Christchurch terror attacks of March 2019, it has been widely acknowledged that news coverage of Islam and Muslim people is another pressing and problematic area of reporting. As Saziah Bashir wrote in the wake of the attacks:

Muslims have been dehumanised and demonised in the media the world over since 9/11. The failure to include Muslim voices in this narrative has left unchallenged the stereotypes painted of us, as if we are a two-dimensional monolith, a single monstrous Other.[149]

There is extensive research literature that demonstrates this point. In his seminal book, *Orientalism*, Edward Said argues that European culture tends to view Arab people and culture as exotic, dangerous and backwards – an uncivilised and threatening 'other' compared to the Western world.[150] This finding has been demonstrated time and again by media researchers. In 2017, a meta-study summarised more than 340 research projects, concluding that Muslims are consistently represented in a negative light, and that Islam is dominantly portrayed as a violent religion.[151]

To give just one example, a UK study analysed the British press coverage of Islam from 2000 to 2008, and found that references to radical Muslims outnumbered references to moderate Muslims by seventeen to one.[152] The idea that Islam is dangerous, backward or irrational was present in 26 per cent of stories. By contrast, only 2 per cent of stories contained the proposition that Muslims supported dominant moral values in British culture. Moreover, the most common nouns used in relation to British Muslims were 'terrorist', 'extremist', 'Islamist', 'suicide bomber' and 'militant', with very few positive nouns (such as 'scholar') used. This is particularly remarkable given that Islam is the second-largest religion in the UK – with more than 2.5 million citizens at the last census.

A 2018 study identified similar trends in the New Zealand media. Researchers analysed stories about Muslims and Islam, and found that reports were far more likely to use the terms 'Islamic terrorism' and 'Islamic Jihad' than they were 'Islam' by itself – suggesting that the majority of stories connect the religion to violence and terrorism.[153]

This negative, stereotypical reporting 'primes' non-Muslim audiences to think of Muslims as a threat. And, indeed, this connection had been drawn before in New Zealand. In 2005, there were six attacks on mosques in Auckland over a two-week period. At the time, Muslim citizens and community leaders pointed to mainstream media coverage as a contributing factor.[154] Writing in the *New Zealand Herald,* Derek Cheng described a town meeting where one attendee commented that news coverage 'bordered on hate speech and promoted the kind of misunderstanding that would have led to the mosque attacks'. Another described a current affairs show item that encouraged viewers to 'hate Muslims and be fearful ... We love New Zealand but it breaks our hearts to see our faith portrayed negatively in the media.'

The reporting on the Christchurch terror attacks was a major break from this reporting pattern, and hopefully has ushered in a new era of more inclusive journalism. The work of many New Zealand journalists and news organisations was held up, around the world, as an example of 'best practice' in reporting on hate crimes. This is because New Zealand journalists, for the most part, declined to give the shooter or his extremist views the 'oxygen of amplification'. This phrase was coined by Whitney Phillips, the author of an important report about journalism, extremism and technology.[155] In the report, Phillips urges reporters to avoid highlighting 'objectively false' ideas and ideologies unless they are prominently undermined or rejected within the article. She also reminds journalists that violent language and memes are 'inherently contagious' and so should not be included without serious thought, context and justification.[156] This advice is supported by research on mass violence that shows shooters often cite previous gunmen as inspiration for their acts of violence.[157]

One study of more than 3,000 articles found that, unlike reporting in Australia, the UK, the US and Canada, the New Zealand media did not name the shooter and it did not focus on his manifesto or ideology.[158] Rather than the perpetrator, New Zealand journalists foregrounded the victims of the attacks, and they focused on the overwhelming community response and messages of unity. The most-read story in the week following the attacks was a set of biographies of all the victims of the shooting by the *New Zealand Herald*, looking at their lives and faith – the article was shared almost 1.4 million times on Facebook.[159]

Importantly, news outlets sought to have New Zealand Muslims' voices centred in the reporting. As one analysis notes:

[It] was a very different perspective of Muslims, Islam and what counts as terrorism than we usually see in Western media. It was inclusive, respectful, nuanced and balanced, and sought to present accurate information from the perspectives of Muslim New Zealanders.[160]

Important conversations have started about the way the media represents Muslims and religious minorities more generally, with some journalists even apologising for the prejudiced articles they had written in the past.[161] This is a very welcome development, and one that hopefully inspires more inclusive, empathetic and diverse reporting on minority groups into the future.

Women in the newsroom

Women are also poorly served by New Zealand mainstream media. There are small pockets of active sexism, such as commentators and hosts who demean women, but the more pervasive issue is a passive or naïve sexism, in which the contribution of women is erased, or media content assumes and perpetuates the idea that women will play a particular, feminine role.

Women make up around 75 per cent of the students on journalism courses in New Zealand, and 50 per cent of the sector more generally. But men often dominate in high-profile positions. Former radio presenter Rachel Smalley raised the issue in 2015, pointing out that six white men dominated prime-time radio at that time:

New Zealand society isn't straight, white and male. So prime time radio, which achieves the greatest audiences, should not be straight, white and male either. It must reflect diversity of perspective, gender and culture. ... No one wins if our world is being shaped by the perspective of one gender and one race.[162]

Male journalists are also, on average, much better paid. In 2015, a large survey of New Zealand journalists found that, although the majority of journalists in New Zealand were women, they were paid 26 per cent less than their male counterparts. Notably, men were paid more even when they held the same position and had the same level of experience.[163]

Men also dominate as sources within the news. Morgan Godfery describes how, during the 2011 election campaign, there were seventy political commentators on New Zealand TV, and only twenty of these were female. There was also a heavy age bias, with not a single commentator, other than Godfery, under forty.[164] These findings are disappointing but, sadly, quite typical around the world. In the UK, men massively outnumber women as experts within the media by about three to one on average. Meanwhile, male reporters and presenters often outnumber women by two to one.[165]

Digital diversity and harassment

Digital media has the power and potential to radically transform the representation of women and minority groups. With the explosion of new media platforms, the traditional gatekeepers (the editors and CEOs running legacy media, who are still overwhelmingly white and male) no longer police access to the public sphere. Just about anyone with the internet can find a platform for their work (and some can find an audience). Social media, podcasts, new websites and digital start-ups have flourished, providing diverse perspectives. In New Zealand, there are excellent websites that foreground progressive, Māori, female and youth voices. To give just one small example, in the lead-up to the 2017 election, *The Spinoff* organised a forum on women under forty in politics – a group that (prior to the election of one as Prime Minister!) were heavily under-represented in political debate.

Another important digital addition is *e-Tangata*,

a weekly digital magazine that publishes New Zealand stories by mostly Māori and Pasifika writers and thinkers, and has been described as focusing on 'big lives, big issues in a conversational style hard to capture in a mainstream media world'. The site is operating on 'the smell of an oily rag', assisted by foundational funding from The Tindall Foundation and the efforts of its founders and wider supporters.[166]

Importantly, when these new outlets and start-ups are successful, they provide a blueprint or 'proof of concept' that commercial outlets can follow. The US podcast 'Another Round', for example, was launched by Buzzfeed as a small side project. The two hosts discuss American culture from the perspective of black women, without apology or attempt to tailor their content to a white audience. It quickly generated a huge following – across diverse demographics – and has shown the commercial potential of a show starring two women of colour.[167] Others have now replicated the success.

Social media and digital news outlets also do important work critiquing the traditional media when they erase minority groups from their coverage or reproduce damaging stereotypes.[168] In Kenya, for example, citizens have used Twitter and the hashtag #SomeoneTellCNN to call out racist and sensationalist news coverage of their country; this led CNN to withdraw some of its more problematic content.[169] We've seen this in New Zealand, too, with backlashes against regressive representation of women and minority groups.[170]

These developments illustrate, as political scientist Andrew Chadwick has argued, that we are living in a 'hybrid media system', where the new and old media are coexisting, and their logic and 'ways of doing things' are feeding into one another. Notably, the logic of digital spaces, which are often full of irreverent, playful commentary as well as more diverse voices, is helping to create more inclusivity and diversity within the traditional media as well.[171]

The transformative potential of new media is exciting. But these new platforms also have a dark and sometimes horrific underbelly: online harassment is rife, and it is targeted at women and minorities in particular. We need to take this seriously or, as more and more journalism moves online, diversity gains may be undermined.

In one of the most disturbing reads of 2016, the *Guardian* published the results of research they had done into 70 million comments left on their news website.[172] The study provided categorical evidence that articles written by women and minorities attract exponentially more abuse and dismissive trolling than those written by white men. Eight of the ten most abused writers were women; the remaining two were black men. The ten writers who got the least abuse were all white men. The frequency of these attacks were unconnected to the subject matter of the articles.

The online attacks on women appear to be at their most vicious when women speak out against sexism. When Canadian-American media critic Anita Sarkeesian pointed out the sexist tropes common in video games, for example, she became the target of a massive online hate campaign, including extensive threats of violence, rape and death. Sarkeesian's Wikipedia profile was vandalised, images of her being raped and beaten were distributed, and she was subject to spamming, hacking, and lobbying of service providers to close her accounts.[173] This response was not an aberration; it is, appallingly, a predictable response to women taking a public stance on issues of gender equality.

Another high-profile example was Caroline Criado-Perez, who received rape and death threats when she campaigned for a woman (other than the Queen) to appear on UK bank notes. And, recently, UK Labour MP Jess Phillips called on the government to take action on the issue after she received more than 600 rape threats in one night.[174]

It's not just political figures either. Cambridge University classicist Mary Beard is often attacked when she does media appearances: a continuation, she argues, of millennia of attempts to silence women in the public sphere.[175] New Zealand's female luminaries often face aggressive criticism when they make public, political statements – from Eleanor Catton to 2013 New Zealander of the Year Dame Anne Salmond and *Whale Rider* star Keisha Castle-Hughes.[176]

The online harassment of women involves what New Zealand researchers have called 'the simultaneous doing and denying of sexism': commenters attack women for speaking out against sexism and, in the process, demonstrate just how real, extensive and scary that sexism is.[177] These researchers looked at 700+ comments posted below news stories about a campaign by Feminist Action against Tui beer for its advertising campaign featuring skimpily dressed women running a brewery. Comments on the articles demonised the feminist campaigners. Some suggested the campaigners must be 'ugly, hairy and fat', lesbians, kill joys and so on. Several 'joked' that the campaigners needed to be raped or sexually dominated.

Megan Whelan is Digital Editor at Radio New Zealand, where she has a front-row seat to audience behaviour. In her experience, 'stories about gender attract abuse, profanity and flat-out nastiness' more than stories on other topics – including those about divisive issues such as politics or the environment.[178] Whelan has systematically reviewed the Facebook comments that readers made on the critically acclaimed podcast series '9th Floor', which profiled New Zealand's former prime ministers. The episodes on Jim Bolger, Mike Moore and Geoffrey Palmer received one abusive comment each. The episode on Jenny Shipley received more than sixty. Whelan notes that '[n]one of the comments appeared to offer any thoughts on her politics, her policies or her actual leadership. Rather, she is called, among other things, a vindictive bitch and a despicable turd.' After writing an article about the sexist nature of these comments, Whelan wryly notes, 'my email was flooded with men telling me how wrong I was'.[179]

Female journalists in New Zealand have described the fear, annoyance, upset and self-doubt these comments cause. The prevailing sense is, 'why do I have to put up with this shit?'[180] As more debate takes place online, journalists and news sources are increasingly exposed to vitriol. This creates a toxic environment for women considering a job in journalism (as well as other parts of public life, such as politics). This landscape also puts women at a distinct disadvantage professionally. One international survey of female technology journalists found that nearly 40 per cent have changed working practices to avoid being targeted by online trolls. One said: 'I've learned how to keep quiet so as to reduce abuse.' Another recounts giving her article to a male colleague to file to escape attacks.[181] Many close their inboxes to strangers, and turn off social media – even though these are important tools for professional journalists. Unless we can find ways to address this harassment, the move online may simply worsen the professional experience of minority and female journalists.

CONCLUSION
This chapter has considered where New Zealand journalism is at its best, and where it is struggling most. It has argued that there is a lack of journalists making independent, critical news on important public issues (what some have called 'democracy reporting' or 'public interest reporting'). This is particularly notable in regional New Zealand, where newspapers, once the lifeblood of their communities, are seeing widespread job cuts and even closures. It has also showed the failure of the news media to capture the diverse experiences of New Zealanders – particularly ethnic minorities and women. The next and final chapter considers how we can address these challenges.

4. LOOKING AHEAD

In one of the most infamous broadcasts of the 1970s, Simon Walker interviewed Prime Minister Robert Muldoon about New Zealand's foreign policy in the Pacific. Muldoon had seen and approved the questions in advance. But halfway through the interview, Walker went off-script and confronted Muldoon with questions he wasn't prepared for. The Prime Minister exploded: 'I will not have some smart alec interviewer changing the rules half way through.'[1]

Four decades later, in 2017, Anika Moa sat down to interview Labour leader Jacinda Ardern in her Auckland home in the run-up to the general election. The conversation was funny, irreverent and deeply personal. It covered Ardern's family background, her favourite character on the TV show *Friends*, and the dildo that was thrown at Steven Joyce's face at Waitangi Day protests in

2016. At one point, the two did impersonations of Helen Clark.[2]

The contrast between the two interviews could hardly be more pronounced and it captures some of the radical changes that have transformed the media landscape over the last forty years. Journalism has become more entertaining, diverse and interactive. The Muldoon-Walker interview was a staid affair: two white men in suits, locked in serious debate. It was broadcast into the lounges of viewers, who consumed it passively, looking to elites as sources of information. The Moa-Ardern interview, by contrast, featured two women, one of whom was Māori, and it was irreverent and informal. It was shown on Māori Television, then available on demand, and distributed on social media, where the audience commented, liked and shared the clip, adding new layers of meaning and interpretation as it was passed around their networks.

Moa's interview may not have delved deeply into policy or political issues, but it likely reached a much wider audience than a 'serious' news report would have, and may therefore have increased political knowledge among some viewers.

These transformations in media production and consumption are dramatic and they require us to re-examine the content and impact of journalism. In this book, I have argued that we should assess journalism in terms of its ability to support democracy. Specifically, we should ask if it is: providing accurate information, holding elites to account, and representing New Zealand in all our diversity.

Using these measuring sticks, we have seen that there is a shortage of critical, professional journalism on matters of public interest, especially in the regions. Addressing these issues will require new business models and new forms of support for journalism. There must also be greater consideration of audiences, to help them navigate the media landscape as informed consumers. Finally, we need to think of ways to address the lack of diversity in our journalism industry, which will require serious reflection and commitment by those running newsrooms up and down the country. This chapter considers these important issues, and where interventions may help, drawing on successful examples from around the world.

MEDIA ECONOMICS

The future for newsprint is uncertain. At most outlets, circulation and advertising revenue continue to drop. And the factors driving this decline are accelerating. The internet is getting faster and cheaper, and every day a greater portion of the population are digital natives – citizens who never developed the habit of reading news offline.

At the start of every year, I ask my students to put their hand up if they pay for a printed newspaper. There are never many. But this year, for the first time since I started lecturing in 2012, not a single hand went up. My students are not apathetic or disinterested – they decided, aged sixteen or seventeen, to study journalism as their full-time degree, so they are among the most news-hungry of their generation. They read multiple publications a day – just not in print.

The number of young people reading print newspapers has been declining for decades,[3] and survey after survey illustrates this online migration.[4] A recent Pew Research Center study analysed news consumption in eight western European countries and found that only 12 per cent of adults aged eighteen to twenty-nine read print newspapers daily.[5]

Given these stark demographic trends, if news-papers are to survive, they will almost all need to move their content online, and try to monetise it.[6]

Over time, it seems that more traditional print journalists are starting to agree. Alan Rusbridger was the editor of the *Guardian* for twenty years, and oversaw the paper's transition from newsprint to a global digital news juggernaut. When the *Guardian* first launched its website, it held back the best stories for the morning newspaper. But over time this morphed into a 'digital-first' strategy.

There was an obvious and compelling reason to put breaking news stories online immediately: audiences wanted information, and if the *Guardian* didn't provide it, another website or social media source would. This logic slowly permeated the newsroom, particularly as website metrics started to show just how big the online readership was. Journalists realised they could reach more people, in a much wider geographic area, through the website, rather than the newspaper.

Eventually all stories were put on the website as soon as they were ready, and the printed paper became a daily curation of the best stories from the website. Rusbridger describes the 2013 publication of the Edward Snowden leaks as a watershed moment: 'For years people had argued you needed print to have impact. But here we were publishing the story with the biggest global impact in the *Guardian*'s 190-year history and we gave no thought to print.'[7] The *Guardian* is now completely global, and its print publication is only a small part of overall operations.

Local and regional newspapers around New Zealand are, of course, very different to a massive global news website like the *Guardian*. For starters, they serve a specific geographic area. This means they can reach their audience with a printed product in a relatively short time span. They also carry less breaking news and more community stories, features and analysis, meaning that timeliness is less important.[8]

But even taking these factors into account, there is no escaping the fact that printing is extremely expensive and inefficient. It is also increasingly hard to justify the environmental cost. As Rusbridger concluded, '[p]lain old words on paper – delivered expensively by essentially Victorian production and distribution methods – couldn't, in the end, compete. The future would be more interactive, more image-driven, more immediate.'[9]

For the time being, printing is justified because of the revenue it brings in. Or – to be more precise – printing is necessary because there is no alternative source of revenue. Most newspapers have not found a way to make money online, and so they rely on this print revenue to survive – even as they watch the figures shrinking in front of them, year on year. Indeed, a recent global estimate suggests that the revenue from print newspapers still accounts for 90 per cent of all income for newspapers around the world.[10]

Some editors in New Zealand are positive about the future of print and believe it will survive.[11] And perhaps it will in some corners.[12] But it is extremely important that we start to make plans for the much more likely scenario that it will not. Huge cuts to journalistic numbers have already happened, and there are few positive signs on the horizon.

Indeed, many commentators believe that newspapers have already waited far too long, wasting valuable time in which they could have been experimenting and innovating while there were still profits in the bank. Roy Greenslade is scathing of what he sees as the 'head in the sand' approach taken by many:

Even before social media, it was obvious that the business model underpinning newspaper publishing could not be sustained. Advertising revenue would continue to decline, and falling sales meant circulation revenue would also drop away. … In such circumstances, if we wanted journalism, as distinct from newspapers, to survive, it was necessary to contemplate new forms of funding.[13]

We do not need newspapers to survive in their printed form. But we do need their underlying journalism. Newspapers have historically done the bulk of democratic reporting: the heavy lifting of discovering, sifting and verifying information. They hire far more journalists than TV and radio, and have been responsible for much more of the day-to-day documentation and questioning of power, and playing the role as a community's 'newspaper of record'. In his book *Losing the News*, Alex S. Jones estimates that, in the US, 85 per cent of accountable journalism has historically been done by newspaper journalists.[14] Moreover, newspaper reports have been vital 'feeders' in the media foodchain, supplying the content on which radio, TV and news websites rely. As the newspaper business model cracks, so too do the foundations of the 'fourth estate'.

There appears to be an emerging consensus that newspapers should not focus their revenue experimentation on digital advertising, because Facebook and Google have, for the time being, won the battle for this market.[15] Most are now experimenting with a mix of revenue streams that include sponsors, side projects (like events or crossword subscriptions), and – most importantly – paying audiences. That means producing journalism for which people are specifically willing to pay – either through cover sales, subscriptions or direct support through donations and memberships.

Rasmus Nielsen, Professor of Political Communication at Oxford University, argues that engaging audiences as a primary source of revenue will require a radical rethink:

For most news organizations, this is a fundamental shift, far more demanding than simply putting up a paywall and hoping people will subscribe. Much of the news currently published online is simply not worth paying for. Some of it is hardly worth our fleeting attention, let alone hard-earned cash.[16]

Journalists need to make a news product that people want to buy; it needs to be helpful or engaging, offering a service of some kind to the audience. But here is the rub. A short update about a council meeting does not always offer a direct service to the individual. Unless you're deeply invested in local politics, it's probably boring. And unless you're directly affected by the issue, it is not necessarily helpful in your life. But the collective benefit of this journalism to society is huge. As we've seen, in this book, the simple presence of a journalist in a council meeting makes elected officials more honest and transparent. Moreover, access to quality journalism leads to higher voter turnout, lower levels of political polarisation among the public, and less corruption. When citizens have access to news they trust, it acts as an immune system, helping to protect society from the danger of disinformation and creeping autocracy. Local news, scrutinising businesses, can even decrease pollution.

In short, it's good for our society. So how can we make sure it is supported? One helpful first step is to raise awareness of the importance of journalism – and the real challenges that newsrooms are facing. With this knowledge, hopefully more people will be willing to support it individually – paying for subscriptions or voluntary memberships, even where they can access content for free. Ideally, the foundations and philanthropists in New Zealand would do the same, creating grants for journalism and news production, as they do elsewhere –

for example, the Pulitzer Center's Open Society Foundation.

Government support

There is also a clear and profound case for the government to support journalism in New Zealand. But government support for journalism needs to be extremely thoughtful. Above all, it needs to protect the independence of journalists. It also needs to take into account the position of commercial actors already operating in the sector, and focus on areas where the market failure is the greatest. Both of these can be achieved with careful policies.

There are three key areas where the government could help.

The first is the least controversial: it can do a lot more to make information transparent and publicly available. All government employees should, as a matter of course, understand their obligations under the Official Information Act, and be trained and resourced to meet these requests quickly. This is arguably one of the single best steps we can take to increase transparency, and help to 'subsidise' journalism by reducing the cost of collecting data.It is also possible to put more data about government activities, spending and public life into the public domain, formatted so that it's easily accessible. And to make it easier for journalists to access elected officials and decision makers – and not just their communications teams. A Radio New Zealand reporter recently posted that it had been more than thirty weeks since the Napier City Council granted her an interview with a staff member, and more than a year since the Hastings District Council did, despite repeated requests. This is an unacceptable delay, and it stands in the way of accountable journalism.[17]

Second, the government can financially support journalism. This support can be indirect – meaning the government subsidises journalism but is not involved in any commissioning or editorial processes. For example, the Canadian Government recently announced a five-year, CA$595 million package that includes: tax rebates for citizens who pay for news subscriptions (incentivising people to pay for news); tax credits for news outlets that produce public interest news (as determined by industry experts); and granting tax-exempt status to non-profit news organisations (making it easier for them to operate as charitable organisations).

Government support for journalism can also be direct – giving money straight to the producers of public interest journalism, for example, through NZ On Air contestable funds, or giving money to Radio New Zealand. As we've seen, New Zealand historically spends very little on its public media, despite having a journalism 'market failure' far bigger than most countries. The countries to which we routinely compare ourselves all have quality public broadcasting on TV. In Australia, the ABC provides TV, radio and online journalism across the country, as does the CBC in Canada, RTE in Ireland and, of course, the BBC in the UK. None of these institutions are without critics. But they are, every one of them, the most trusted provider of news and information in their respective countries: and this is true among voters from across the political spectrum. A recent survey in Australia, for example, found:

[P]eople trust the ABC more than any other news source and would like to see it given more money. ... Support was strong among voters regardless of party allegiances with 76 per cent of Coalition voters in favour of the ABC being protected ... 74 per cent of Labor voters and 87 per cent of Greens voters.[18]

Significantly, the second-most trusted news sources in these countries is often a long, long way behind the public service broadcaster. A recent poll in the UK, for example, found that 58 per cent of respondents ranked the BBC in first place for balanced and unbiased reporting. Sky News was second on the list at only 15 per cent.[19] And in a survey of more than 8,000 Americans, Michael Kearney, Assistant Professor of Journalism at the Missouri School of Journalism, found that US public TV and National Public Radio were the only American news outlets to appear in the top five 'most trusted media' list. The remainder were actually British.[20] Not a single commercial outlet made the top five.

Government support should focus on the content that the commercial media is failing to produce. We've seen, through this book, that local and regional journalism is highly at risk, whereas national reporting, analysis and commentary are less so. So this should be prioritised.

In the UK, an £8 million scheme aims to rebuild reporting on local government, by funding 150 'local democracy reporters'. Supported by the BBC licence fee (the annual charge paid by every household with a TV), small news publishers can apply for the scheme, which pays the salary of additional local reporters to work at their organisation. In return for the financing, newspapers cannot use the new positions as an opportunity to cut newsroom staff, and they must assign the reporters to cover local government beats. The news they write is then shared through wire service with newspapers, radio stations, TV broadcasters and news websites around the country.[21]

Some have argued this is only a temporary band-aid in a wider landscape of closures and redundancies.[22] But it has, nonetheless, resulted in far more original journalism about local issues and politics: in the first year of the scheme, local democracy reporters filed 50,000 stories.[23] Matthew

Barraclough, head of local news partnerships at the BBC, notes:

[I]n some parts of the UK the Local Democracy Reporter may be the only journalist closely following council business. Their scrutiny not only serves the public interest, it supports the councils themselves. These reporters highlight successes as well [as] problems, and they make the decisions of local authorities interesting and relevant to the electorate.[24]

Inspired by the BBC's scheme, New Zealand has launched a small $1 million pilot that will see eight journalists providing 'local democracy news' for syndication to a range of media. The goal of this scheme is to 'fill gaps in the reporting of local bodies and other publicly-funded organisations, mostly in regional New Zealand, brought about by significant decreases in reporting numbers in traditional media'.[25] There is not yet any indication of whether the scheme will be expanded or renewed: there was no money for it in the 2019 Budget.[26]

Local democracy reporters will not solve all the problems facing journalism, but they are a creative way to support existing news outlets (both commercial and not for profit) at a relatively low cost. The pilot should be rigorously evaluated and, if it is working well, scaled up. Ultimately, this could also be built up into a newswire or shared news service resembling the now closed NZPA – pooling news from around the country, as well as making original content. This might also include journalists who would work to 'localise' international issues and events for a New Zealand audience. Such a news service could be set up independently, or perhaps in cooperation with Radio New Zealand, which has a nationwide network of correspondents, and has already started to share its content with other news organisations.

Journalist Tess McClure, who has researched strategies to support local journalism, points out that if this scheme was implemented in the next few years, it could also take advantage of the existing regional local reporters who are currently facing the spectre of paper sales and redundancy – and preserve some of that institutional knowledge before it disappears entirely.[27]

Government support for journalism through schemes like this will be crucial if more news outlets follow the lead of the *New Zealand Herald* and put their news behind a subscription paywall. In that scenario, there would be a rise in 'information in-equality' online, where only those who could afford the subscription would have access to information. Openly available, shared journalism would be even more important to supporting a fair society.

The third and final area where the government plays an important role is probably the most difficult to get right: making sure that the media industry as a whole is fit for purpose, and fair.

That involves checking that there is adequate competition (so there is a plurality of views), as well as supporting collaboration to help address market failures. It also means working out how to govern the large technology companies that provide the information architecture in which we now operate. How the government decides to regulate (or not) Google and Facebook has giant implications for the future of the journalism industry.

This needs to be done using evidence – we still do not understand the extent to which our news flows are manipulated on these platforms. And it should be done with an eye to creating a fair and open playing field. When platform companies act as news providers (curating, producing, editing and publishing their own news and profiting from this), then they should be held to the same standard as our own journalists – which means paying taxes, following the media law of New Zealand, and being held to ethical standards.

MEDIA LITERACY

The production of quality journalism is only one piece of the puzzle. With vast quantities of poor information online, and ever-evolving technology, it is also important that audiences have the skills to navigate the media ecosystem, so they can parse the credible from the misleading.

Individuals need to take on more responsibility

than they have in the past. Claire Wardle is the director of First Draft, an organisation working to address trust and truth issues in the digital landscape. She has written extensively on the challenges of disinformation and trust in media. Wardle argues that individuals must check themselves, particularly when they use social media:

Every time we passively accept information without double-checking, or share a post, image or video before we've verified it, we're adding to the noise and confusion. The ecosystem is now so polluted, we have to take responsibility for independently checking what we see online ... this is about teaching people to second guess their instinctual reactions. If you find yourself incredibly angry at a piece of content or feeling smug (because your viewpoint has been reaffirmed), take another look.[28]

Not many people know how to check the information they encounter. Moreover, our brains use a number of unhelpful shortcuts to help us process the information.[29] These are not neutral: we have a very strong preference for 'facts' that confirm our existing beliefs. This confirmation bias (or what researchers Hugo Mercier and Dan Sperber call 'myside bias'[30]) means that we tend to dismiss evidence that contradicts our core beliefs. We also love being right; we experience genuine pleasure – a rush of dopamine – when we are processing information that supports our beliefs.[31]

Cumulatively, these quirks mean that it can be

very difficult to counter false information with true information. In fact, in some cases, trying to correct misinformation has been shown to make people double down on their false beliefs – a phenomenon known as the 'backfire effect'. One research study found that, in the lead-up to the Iraq war in 2003, self-identified conservatives became more likely to believe that Iraq had weapons of mass destruction after reading that none existed.

In another study, participants were shown information confirming that there was a scientific consensus that humans have caused global warming. This information caused some of the study's participants – those with a strong belief in the free market – to become less accepting of the idea that humans have caused climate change.[32] It was seemingly easier for these participants to believe that there was a scientific cover-up or mistake than it was to accept information that might conflict with their core political belief (that is, that we might need to intervene in the free market to stop humans damaging the environment).[33]

Frustratingly, even when we succeed in correcting false beliefs, the false information continues to influence our thoughts and actions. In one study, a group of participants were shown an article about a married woman who stole drugs from the hospital where she worked. The study participants were asked to evaluate the woman on several dimensions, including trustworthiness. They were then told that the article had contained an error and the woman had not stolen the drugs, and were asked to evaluate her again. The participants revised their evaluations, but they were not as high as those of a control group who had never learned the false information. The researchers concluded that 'the influence of incorrect information cannot simply be undone by pointing out that this information was incorrect'.[34] The damage was already done.

So what can we do? How do we support audiences navigating this online world, and establish who they can trust? We do not have a big 'fake news' problem in New Zealand, and we are unlikely to develop one. But we do have a lot of mistrust in journalism, which makes audiences vulnerable to influence from polemical commentators who dismiss evidence, or from more global sources of misinformation, particularly about health and the environment.

It's easy to teach students technical fact-checking skills – these classes already exist. They tend to focus on 'lateral verification' – that is, encouraging students to search sideways to check the authenticity and reliability of a website: examining its URL, online footprint, social media presence, references to it in other locations, and so on. Conceptually, this is not dissimilar to how we encourage students of history to verify sources in the archives – before taking the claims of an individual or organisation into account, you should ensure that it is reliable. A recent, large-scale experiment found that these skills – knowledge of internet and production processes – are strongly correlated with the ability of users to tell a fake news image from a real one.[35] The study asked more than 3,000 respondents to assess the credibility of images attached to news stories. Some of the images were faked, doctored and edited, while others were not. The study found (not surprisingly) that the respondents' internet skills, photo-editing experience and social media experience were good predictors of whether they could tell a fake image from a real one. The authors concluded that 'to mitigate the potential harm caused by fake images online, the best strategy is investing in educational efforts to increase users' digital media literacy'.[36]

Unfortunately, these technical strategies also date rapidly as digital technology advances. So, more broadly, we need to focus curricula on the critical thinking skills that underpin verification, regardless of the platform.

Recent research has shown these interventions can be massively beneficial to a student's ability to distinguish opinion and fact. In 2016, Allen Nsangi and her colleagues ran a huge trial involving

10,000 school children in 120 primary schools in Kampala, Uganda. One group of students, aged ten to twelve, were given a comic book and a series of lessons about critical thinking and fact verification. These covered twelve key concepts, such as the importance of using scientific methods (like randomised control trials) to establish facts, and information about common errors people make in their reasoning (like confusing an anecdote with evidence).[37] The results, which were published in *The Lancet*, showed that the kids who were taught basic concepts about critical thinking massively outperformed the others in a series of scenario-based tests assessing false claims: 69 per cent of the students who had done the class passed, compared to only 27 per cent of the control group.

Education strategies like this will play a crucial role in the global response to misinformation. Finland has been deemed 'most resilient to disinformation' according to the Media Literacy Index, compiled by the Open Society Institute in Sofia – an award directly attributed to its extensive media literacy education in schools, which includes critical thinking skills and technical classes.[38]

Legislators in California are currently considering a bill that would embed more media literacy into the curricula there, as well as provide media literacy training for teachers.[39] Meanwhile, the European Commission's High Level Expert

Group for fake news and online disinformation has made a key recommendation that member countries 'promote media and information literacy to counter disinformation and help users navigate the digital media environment'.[40] The UK has recently acted on this recommendation, and from 2020, children in primary school and secondary school will learn what 'fake news' is, and how to spot it. Classes will cover ideas including: what confirmation bias is; how to recognise techniques used for persuasion; and how to evaluate what they see online, and identify risks.[41]

News organisations can also do more to help audiences navigate their journalism. One important step is to increase transparency by making the source of news more obvious – especially when it is repurposed from newswires, press releases or sponsored content. Sponsored content, in particular, should be made extremely clear to the reader. Too often the tag explaining a story's provenance appears in a tiny font at the bottom or top of the page, while the remainder of the article is formatted to look exactly like a news story. It is no surprise that 80 per cent of US middle school children cannot distinguish this 'native advertising' from real news content (and, of course, this is exactly why advertisers pay for this format). This can lead to only two outcomes, both of which undermine trust in the media: either the reader is tricked into thinking the paid advert is journalism, or the reader notices the small print and feels the outlet is trying to deceive them.

MEDIA DIVERSITY

Finally, there is important work to be done in supporting public debate, and diversity in particular. This is an extremely challenging issue, as it is intertwined with wider cultural trends and policy issues: unconscious bias, parental leave, social convention and more. But at the very least, we can work to draw attention to the problem, and create clear incentives for media outlets to take this issue seriously.

In the UK, a very effective intervention has been run by the Women on Air group, who monitor the ratio of male and female journalists and experts who appear on prominent TV news bulletins.[42] Every year, the research team publicly announce their results at a conference with leading industry figures. The news editors of Channel 4, BBC, ITV and Sky have all acknowledged that this monitoring makes them think harder about the culture in their newsrooms, and what they can do to diversify content. In just a couple of years, the overall ratio of women experts across the main broadcasters has gone up from 3:1 to 2:1.[43] The same approach could help to shine a spotlight on the gap in the New Zealand media for Māori, Pasifika and women journalists and sources – 'naming and shaming' the worst media offenders and celebrating those who have made progress.

Again, technology may help here. The *Financial Times* has developed an app that automatically monitors the gender of sources quoted within news stories. This was introduced after a study showed that only 21 per cent of people quoted in that publication were women. The bot uses pronouns and analysis of first names to determine whether a source is male or female, with the goal of pushing back against the implicit bias of journalists.[44]

In 2019, it should be embarrassing to have an entire room of men writing about gender issues, or an entire room of Pākehā writing on race relations. Of course, it's possible for journalists to do an excellent job reporting on topics of which they have no personal experience. But – as with any other domain of human practice – they can also have blindspots, succumb to groupthink (when group members refrain from disagreeing with the consensus), or simply miss things out. Examples of this have been well documented. One research study found that male journalists were far more likely to automatically use male sources in their stories.[45] Another has shown that journalists in Washington overwhelmingly retweet the news from other male journalists, and ignore that of female journalists.[46] Another showed that male newsroom editors were less likely to consider issues around parenting and maternity, making it harder for journalists who become mothers to stay in the newsroom.[47]

Finally, newsrooms must support their employees as they deal with online harassment. This abuse can inflict a serious emotional and professional toll. Charlotte Graham-McLay, who has researched the harassment of female journalists in New Zealand, found that almost no newsrooms had policies in place to support or protect their employees against harassment, even though it is a daily occurrence.[48] Unless we can find ways to address this and take it seriously, the move online may worsen the professional experience for female and minority journalists, undermining our steps towards greater media diversity.

CONCLUSION

Around the world, the news media is under attack. According to UNESCO, 2018 was the deadliest year on record for journalists: at least 99 were killed, a further 348 imprisoned and 60 held hostage.[49] These attacks are not confined to countries run by dictators or ravaged by conflict. In Europe, the supposed birthplace of the free press, journalists have been killed in Malta, Northern Ireland, Bulgaria and Slovakia over the last two years.

In addition to this violence, politicians

worldwide are attacking the media, trying to delegitimise critical reporting in the eyes of the public, and sowing seeds of doubt and mistrust.

In July 2019, the UK convened the largest ever gathering of politicians and ministers committed to supporting media freedom.[50] Human rights lawyer Amal Clooney, the head of a newly formed international panel of legal experts working to protect journalists, told the crowd: 'Silencing of information is happening at levels never seen before. The way the world responds to this crisis will define our generation and determine whether democracy can survive.'[51]

Alongside the violent attacks, misinformation and declining revenue for the news industry, there is some good news. A host of governments have taken action, launching support packages for journalism and media literacy training programmes. More generally, audiences are waking up to the value of journalism, and the need to be cautious with whom they trust online. In the 2019 Reuters *Digital News Report*, 24 per cent of respondents said that, compared to a year ago, they have started to rely on reputable news brands and stopped using sources with 'less accurate' reputations; 41 per cent said they checked the accuracy of reports by comparing multiple sources.[52]

Technological advances mean that we can also do more journalism with fewer resources than ever before: my students have more power and capability on their cell phones than many newsrooms had forty years ago. They can create and edit professional, multimedia packages on the go.

And while there is more misinformation, there are also huge troves of data that, in the right hands, can be used to discover, authenticate and verify information like never before.

In July 2018, a shocking video circulated on social media showing a small group of women and children being blindfolded and shot in an unknown location in West Africa. The video was allegedly filmed in Cameroon, but the country's Minister of Communications dismissed it as 'fake news'. However, the BBC's *Africa Eye* programme, working with Amnesty International and the investigative network Bellingcat, launched a crowd sourced investigation. Taking images from the video and cross-referencing them with Google Earth satellite images, public documents and archives, the investigation was able to pinpoint precisely where and when the shootings took place, and the names of the likely killers.[53] As a result, seven Cameroonian soldiers were arrested, and the US withdrew over US$17 million in 'security aid' to Cameroon.

This remarkable investigation illustrates the power of journalism, harnessing technology, to hold power to account. Reflecting on the open source, evidence-based investigation, the *New York Review of Books* wrote:

This is the closest that journalism has come to a scientific method: the transparency allows the process to be replicated, the underlying data to be examined, and the conclusions to be tested by others. This is worlds apart from the journalism of assertion that demands trust in expert authority ... Journalism badly needs this infusion of vitality and credibility.[54]

In New Zealand, we are fortunate that we do not have to deal with violence towards the media, or political elites who routinely attack journalists. But we are confronting an intense economic crisis that raises questions about the ability of journalists to continue doing their job of supporting democracy, and holding elites to account. Advertising revenue has fallen away, and local news outlets, in particular, are struggling to survive.

We don't know what will come next in the media. As media scholar Chris Anderson writes: '[N]ews is simultaneously dying and being reborn. We don't know yet what economic models of journalistic production will emerge from the rubble of the industrial news age.'[55]

It is possible that journalists, philanthropists, businesses and communities will band together, supported by new technologies, and develop a new model for quality local journalism. But we should not take this for granted. It is equally possible that what emerges from the rubble will be increasingly fragmented and ad hoc content that fails to shed light on important issues or scrutinise those in power.

This would be a devastating development for our political system. The most important and challenging issues of our times – extremism, climate change, poverty, housing and migration, to name just a few – require us to examine evidence, and have open debates about our values and the competing interests that are at stake. We need to support the production of professional, independent journalism where the market is failing to.

Since the 2008 global financial crisis, it is common to hear the phrase 'too big to fail'. It refers to the idea that certain financial institutions are so large that their failure would be disastrous to the wider economic system. They must, therefore, be supported by government if they face potential ruin. There is a parallel in journalism. But rather than being too big to fail, journalism is too important. Its failure would be disastrous for the wider political system on which everything else is built.

NOTES

Introduction

1   Kathy Frankovic, 'Belief in conspiracies largely depends on political identity', YouGov, 27 December 2016, https://today.yougov.com/topics/politics/articles-reports/2016/12/27/belief-conspiracies-largely-depends-political-iden (accessed 8 June 2018).

2   Reporters Without Borders, '2019 World Press Freedom Index – A cycle of fear', https://rsf.org/en/2019-world-press-freedom-index-cycle-fear (accessed 27 July 2019).

3   Merja Myllylahti, *New Zealand Media Ownership 2018*, AUT Research Centre for Journalism, Media and Democracy, December 2018, www.aut.ac.nz/__data/assets/pdf_file/0013/231511/JMAD-2018-Report.pdf (accessed 21 January 2019).

4   Erin McKenzie, 'Public relations vs journalism: Is the rise of PR a threat to the fourth estate?', *StopPress*, 1 December 2015, http://stoppress.co.nz/news/public-service-journalism-versus-public-relations-professionals-uprising-pr-threatening-fourth-estate (accessed 9 June 2018).

5   In the US, by contrast, there has been an estimated 40 per cent reduction in newspaper journalists since 2006. Rick Edmonds, 'Newspaper industry lost 3,800 full-time editorial professionals in 2014', *Poynter*, 28 July 2015, www.poynter.org/reporting-editing/2015/newspaper-industry-lost-3800-full-time-editorial-professionals-in-2014 (accessed 8 June 2018).

6   In the 2006 Census, 4,044 New Zealanders classified themselves as journalists, while in 2013, this figure had dropped to 3,603 – an 11 per cent decrease. In addition, digital news start-ups tend to be based in urban centres, rather than the regions, where there have been some of the biggest cuts to newspaper journalists. See Jack Shafer and Tucker Doherty, 'The media bubble is worse than you think', *Politico Magazine*, May/June 2017, www.politico.com/magazine/

story/2017/04/25/media-bubble-real-journalism-jobs-east-coast-215048 (accessed 17 January 2019).

7   Chris Barton, 'Anatomy of a redundancy: The suffocation of long-form journalism in New Zealand', in Emma Johnson, Giovanni Tiso, Sarah Illingworth and Barnaby Bennett (eds), *Don't Dream It's Over: Reimagining Journalism in Aotearoa New Zealand*, Freerange Press, Christchurch, 2016, p.146.

8   Professor Barbie Zelizer at the University of Pennsylvania makes a related point, arguing that the consistent reference to a 'media crisis' and a 'crisis' in journalism obscures more than it illuminates. Zelizer argues that we should, instead, interrogate and differentiate between the 'diverse set of technological, political, economic, social, occupational, moral and legal circumstances' journalists operate within today. Barbie Zelizer, 'Terms of choice: Uncertainty, journalism, and crisis', *Journal of Communication*, 65, 5 (2015), pp.888–908, https://doi.org/10.1111/jcom.12157 (accessed 19 July 2019).

9   For a further discussion, see Heidi Tworek and John Maxwell Hamilton, 'Why the "golden age" of newspapers was the exception, not the rule', Nieman Lab, 2 May 2018, www.niemanlab.org/2018/05/why-the-golden-age-of-newspapers-was-the-exception-not-the-rule (accessed 10 January 2019). Taking the long view, media historians tend to see periods of consistent, quality journalism as the exception rather than the rule: for example, Andrew Pettegree, *The Invention of News: How the World Came to Know about Itself*, Yale University Press, New Haven, CT, 2014.

10 '"The Arrangements": A work of fiction', *New York Times*, 28 June 2016, www.nytimes.com/2016/07/03/books/review/melania-trump-in-chimamanda-ngozi-adichie-short-story.html (accessed 9 June 2018).

11 'Ta-Nehisi Coates', *Atlantic*, www.theatlantic.com/author/ta-nehisi-coates (accessed 1 August 2019).

12 To name just a few recent examples: Stuff's commitment to climate change reporting in its series *Quick! Save the planet*, as well as its multimedia project on the Treaty of Waitangi; Radio New

Zealand's '9th Floor' podcast series, interviewing former prime ministers; a number of brilliant investigations from *Newsroom*; Toby Morris's political cartoons that have gone viral around the world; and sharp analysis and satire on *The Spinoff*. There are numerous other examples, some of which are detailed in the pages of this book. For a recent roundup of great pieces, see Alex Braae, 'The best NZ journalism of 2018, as chosen by you', *The Spinoff*, 21 December 2018, https://thespinoff.co.nz/the-bulletin/21-12-2018/the-best-nz-journalism-of-2018-as-chosen-by-you (accessed 18 July 2019). As well as the list of annual Voyager Media Awards winners.

13 Phone interview with Gavin Ellis, 21 April 2017.

14 See the Acknowledgements for names of those I spoke with.

15 In New Zealand's case, journalism very literally preceded democracy. Newspapers were published here from 1840 onwards – before self-government began and decades before universal suffrage. Indeed, newspapers played an important role in advocating for independence, and the expansion of voting rights. For a discussion of this early period, see Ian F. Grant, *Lasting Impressions: The Story of New Zealand Newspapers, 1840–1920*, Fraser Books in association with the Alexander Turnbull Library, Wellington, 2018.

Chapter 1

1 Gardiner Harris and Melissa Eddy, 'Obama, with Angela Merkel in Berlin, assails spread of fake news', *New York Times*, 17 November 2016, www.nytimes.com/2016/11/18/world/europe/obama-angela-merkel-donald-trump.html (accessed 9 June 2018).

2 Amy Mitchell, Jesse Holcomb and Michael Barthel, 'Many Americans believe fake news is sowing confusion', Pew Research Center, 15 December 2016, www.journalism.org/2016/12/15/many-americans-believe-fake-news-is-sowing-confusion (accessed 9 June 2018).

3 Jay Rosen, 'Winter is coming: Prospects for the American press under Trump', PressThink, 28 December 2016, http://pressthink.org/2016/12/winter-coming-prospects-american-press-trump (accessed 28 August 2017).

4   Margaret Sullivan, 'It's time to retire the tainted term "fake news"', *Washington Post*, 8 January 2017, www.washingtonpost.com/lifestyle/style/its-time-to-retire-the-tainted-term-fake-news/2017/01/06/a5a7516c-d375-11e6-945a-76f69a399dd5_story.html?utm_term=.c95810ddefc2 (accessed 19 July 2019).

5   See, for example, Claire Wardle, 'Fake news. It's complicated', *First Draft*, 16 February 2017, https://firstdraftnews.org/fake-news-complicated (accessed 10 June 2018).

6   David Uberti, 'The real history of fake news', *Columbia Journalism Review*, 15 December 2016, www.cjr.org/special_report/fake_news_history.php (accessed 19 May 2018).

7   Onora O'Neill, 'A Question of Trust', The Reith Lectures, BBC, 2002, www.bbc.co.uk/programmes/p00ghvd8 (accessed 8 June 2018).

8   From John Milton, *Areopagitica: A Speech of Mr. John Milton for the Liberty of Unlicensed Printing, to the Parliament of England*, London, 1644.

9   John Stuart Mill, *On Liberty*, Penguin Classics, London, 1974, p.33.

10 S. Vosoughi, D. Roy and S. Aral, 'The spread of true and false news online', *Science*, 359, 6380 (9 March 2018), pp.1146–51, https://doi.org/10.1126/science.aap9559 (accessed 19 July 2019). Another study looked at information spread in a specific US community, and found that real news, and what the researchers call 'junk news', were shared in equal ratios: 'Social media users in Michigan shared a lot of political content, but the amount of professionally researched political news and information was consistently smaller than the amount of extremist, sensationalist, conspiratorial, masked commentary, fake news and other forms of junk news. … Not only did such junk news "outperform" real news, but the proportion of professional news content being shared hit its lowest point the day before the election.' Philip Howard et al., 'Junk news and bots during the U.S. election: What were Michigan voters sharing over Twitter?', COMPROP Data Memo 2017.1, 26 March 2017, http://comprop.oii.ox.ac.

uk/wp-content/uploads/
sites/89/2017/03/What-Were-
Michigan-Voters-Sharing-
Over-Twitter-v2.pdf (accessed
16 January 2019).

11   Hunt Allcott and Matthew
      Gentzkow, 'Social media
      and fake news in the 2016
      election', *Journal of Economic
      Perspectives*, 31, 2 (2017),
      pp.211–36, https://web.
      stanford.edu/~gentzkow/
      research/fakenews.pdf
      (accessed 19 July 2019).

12   2,200 children were shown
      a 'fake news quiz' containing
      six stories, two of which were
      false. The sample included
      both primary school children
      and secondary school
      students, who were shown
      different, age-appropriate
      versions of the stories. In both
      groups, girls performed better
      than boys, reflecting the more
      general literacy gap between
      the genders at this age; and
      high-income students did
      better than children from low-
      income families. The National
      Literacy Trust, 'Fake news
      and critical literacy: The final
      report of the Commission on
      Fake News and the Teaching
      of Critical Literacy in Schools',
      compiled by the National
      Literacy Trust, June 2018,
      https://literacytrust.org.uk/
      research-services/research-
      reports/fake-news-and-
      critical-literacy-final-report
      (accessed 19 July 2019).

13   Quoted in Heather Bryant,
      'The universe of people trying
      to deceive journalists keeps
      expanding, and newsrooms
      aren't ready', Nieman Lab, 19
      July 2018, www.niemanlab.
      org/2018/07/the-universe-
      of-people-trying-to-deceive-
      journalists-keeps-expanding-
      and-newsrooms-arent-ready
      (accessed 20 January 2019).

14   Franklin Foer, 'Reality's End',
      Atlantic, May 2018, www.
      theatlantic.com/magazine/
      archive/2018/05/realitys-
      end/556877 (accessed 19 July
      2019).

15   Studies of social media
      during the riots concluded
      that Twitter was surprisingly
      good at identifying and
      shutting down false claims.
      See Jonathan Richards and
      Paul Lewis, 'How Twitter was
      used to spread – and knock
      down – rumours during the
      riots', *Guardian*, 7 December
      2011, www.theguardian.
      com/uk/2011/dec/07/how-
      twitter-spread-rumours-riots
      (accessed 21 January 2019).

16   There are high levels of trust
      in the BBC, compared to
      other news outlets in the UK:

see BBC, 'Public perceptions of the impartiality and trustworthiness of the BBC', survey, November 2017, https://downloads.bbc.co.uk/aboutthebbc/insidethebbc/howwework/reports/pdf/bbc_report_trust_and_impartiality_nov_2017.pdf (accessed 21 January 2019). This is not to say that their reporting on the riots was necessarily good. Many have argued that news outlets in the UK were far too accepting of police reports, dismissive of protesters' and rioters' serious concerns about police brutality, and were reproducing racist stereotypes. The point here is just that, on the nights when things were unfolding, news outlets including the BBC played an important role in checking and verifying claims, letting people know which areas were safe and so on.

17   Art Swift, 'Americans' trust in mass media sinks to new low', Gallup, 14 September 2016, http://news.gallup.com/poll/195542/americans-trust-mass-media-sinks-new-low.aspx (accessed 9 June 2018).

18   Jonathan M. Ladd, *Why Americans Hate the Media and How It Matters*, Princeton University Press, Princeton, NJ, 2012.

19   Jeremy Peters, 'Wielding claims of "fake news," conservatives take aim at mainstream media', *New York Times*, 25 December 2016, www.nytimes.com/2016/12/25/us/politics/fake-news-claims-conservatives-mainstream-media-.html (accessed 10 June 2018).

20   Margaret L. Taylor, 'Combating disinformation and foreign interference in democracies: Lessons from Europe', Brookings, 31 July 2019, www.brookings.edu/blog/techtank/2019/07/31/combating-disinformation-and-foreign-interference-in-democracies-lessons-from-europe (accessed 14 August 2019); Simin Kargar, 'It's not just the Russians anymore as Iranians turn up disinformation efforts ahead of 2020 vote', *Washington Post*, 25 July 2019, www.washingtonpost.com/technology/2019/07/25/its-not-just-russians-anymore-iranians-others-turn-up-disinformation-efforts-ahead-vote (accessed 14 August 2019).

21   Some have suggested that

China may seek to influence New Zealand perceptions through propaganda. Anne-Marie Brady, 'Magic weapons: China's political influence activities under Xi Jinping', Kissinger Institute on China and the United States, Wilson Center, Washington, DC, 18 September 2017, www.wilsoncenter.org/article/magic-weapons-chinas-political-influence-activities-under-xi-jinping (accessed 21 January 2019).

22 Acumen Republic and Edelman, 'The battle for truth: 2018 Acumen Edelman Trust Barometer', www.acumenrepublic.com/media/1406/trust-barometer-new-zealand-march-2018.pdf (accessed 19 July 2019).

23 Some of this research is collected on: London School of Economics, 'Journalism credibility: Strategies to restore trust', www.lse.ac.uk/media-and-communications/truth-trust-and-technology-commission/journalism-credibility (accessed 21 January 2019).

24 Maxwell T. Boykoff and Jules M. Boykoff, 'Balance as bias: Global warming and the US prestige press', *Global Environmental Change*, 14 (2004), pp.125–36, www.eci.ox.ac.uk/publications/downloads/boykoff04-gec.pdf (accessed 19 July 2019).

25 It should be noted that many are now actively trying to work to bridge this partisanship and alter their reporting practices by, for example, hiring more diverse opinion writers, and being more transparent in their journalistic practices. There are also news outlets springing up to try to bring groups together in dialogue. See, for example, Eduardo Suárez, 'Four news startups trying to improve civic discourse', Nieman Reports, 27 June 2018, https://niemanreports.org/articles/four-news-startups-trying-to-improve-civic-discourse (accessed 21 January 2019).

26 Mike Hosking, 'Closing monologue', *Seven Sharp*, TV One, 1 April 2014.

27 See, for example, Toby Manhire, '"I'm completely squeaky clean": An interview with Matthew Hooton', *The Spinoff*, 10 January 2019, https://thespinoff.co.nz/politics/10-01-2019/im-completely-squeaky-clean-an-interview-with-matthew-hooton (accessed 20 January 2019); Ian Shirley, 'Opinion is

killing journalism', *Pundit*, 11 December 2017, www.pundit.co.nz/content/opinion-is-killing-journalism (accessed 20 January 2019); and Roger Horrocks, 'A short history of the New Zealand intellectual', in *Re-inventing New Zealand: Essays on the Arts and the Media*, Atuanui Press, Waikato, 2016, p.148.

28 A different, less problematic form of sponsorship involves an advertiser (or philanthropist) sponsoring a whole section of a publication or programme – for example, the Bill & Melinda Gates Foundation pays for a section on international development in the *Guardian*. This can lead to perceived conflicts of interest (for example, when a *Guardian* journalist reports on a Gates-funded development project). But, done carefully, with editorial autonomy protected, it can also be a vital way to support the production of important news that would not otherwise be made. I've written more about this issue in: Mel Bunce, 'Foundations, philanthropy and international journalism', *Ethical Space: The International Journal of Communication Ethics*, 13,
2/3 (2016), pp.6–15, http://openaccess.city.ac.uk/id/eprint/13498 (accessed 3 August 2019).

29 Sam Wineburg, Sarah McGrew, Joel Breakstone and Teresa Ortega, 'Evaluating information: The cornerstone of civic online reasoning', Stanford Digital Repository, 2016, http://purl.stanford.edu/fv751yt5934 (accessed 30 September 2018).

30 Making things even more complicated, some of the platforms have decided to treat certain promoted news stories as though they are not just adverts, but political adverts. The News Media Alliance, in conjunction with other media organisations, has warned this may further undermine trust in journalism: 'Placing news ads in an archive designed to capture political advertising [is] another step toward furthering a false and dangerous narrative that blurs the lines between real reporting from the professional media and propaganda.' News Media Alliance, letter to Mark Zuckerberg, CEO of Facebook, 18 May 2018, www.newsmediaalliance.org/wp-content/uploads/2018/05/FB-

Political-Ads-Letter-FINAL. pdf (accessed 19 July 2019).

31 Even the celebrated ideal of the journalist as an 'objective' and 'impartial' witness (rather than a polemicist) was an invention designed to sell more newspapers. Objectivity emerged in the mid-1800s, largely as a way to help news outlets and newswires sell their journalism to a wider range of people and publications, regardless of political persuasion. See James T. Hamilton, *All the News That's Fit to Sell: How the Market Transforms Information into News*, Princeton University Press, Princeton, NJ, 2003; and Jean Chalaby, *The Invention of Journalism*, Palgrave Macmillan, Basingstoke, 1998.

32 This is the overall average; at some outlets, there has been a significant increase in revenue from digital content. See Joshua Benton, 'The New York Times is on pace to earn more than $600 million in digital this year, halfway to its ambitious goal', Nieman Lab, 1 November 2018, www. niemanlab.org/2018/11/ the-new-york-times-is-on-pace-to-earn-more-than-600-million-in-digital-this-year-halfway-to-its-ambitious-goal (accessed 7 January 2018).

33 Mark Derby, 'Newspapers', Te Ara – the Encyclopedia of New Zealand, http://www. TeAra.govt.nz/en/newspapers (accessed 14 August 2019).

34 These platforms also have access to huge swathes of data that can make advertising very targeted and effective, for example, displaying adverts based on demographics, personal search history, purchases, social media behaviour, friendship group, and much more. In fact, the customer data is so detailed, and the advertising is so specific, that it's not uncommon for people to think their smartphones are recording them. Why else would Facebook show you an ad for the perfume your mum literally just asked about at lunch? Answer: because she searched for the perfume online but didn't buy it. Facebook knows you're related and currently in the same physical location. This example was one of many on the fascinating podcast 'Reply All', Episode #109: Is Facebook Spying on You?, Gimlet, 2 November 2017, www.gimletmedia.com/

reply-all/109-facebook-spying (accessed 8 June 2018).

35 Ben Bold, 'Google and Facebook to command nearly 65% of UK online ad market by 2021', Campaign, 26 March 2019, www.campaignlive.co.uk/article/google-facebook-command-nearly-65-uk-online-ad-market-2021/1580126 (accessed 30 July 2019).

36 Mathew Ingram, 'How Google and Facebook have taken over the digital ad industry', *Fortune*, 4 January 2017, http://fortune.com/2017/01/04/google-facebook-ad-industry (accessed 21 January 2019). See also PWC, 'Media businesses and advertisers struggle to keep up with changing audience behaviour', press release, 8 May 2017, www.pwc.co.nz/news-releases/2017-news-releases/2017-05-08-media-businesses-advertisers-struggle-to-keep-up.html (accessed 28 December 2018).

37 Jonathan Underhill, 'Merged Fairfax, NZME would have just 12% of NZ digital and market dominated by Google, Facebook', *National Business Review*, 27 May 2016, www.nbr.co.nz/article/merged-fairfax-nzme-would-have-just-12-nz-digital-ad-market-dominated-google-facebook-b (accessed 12 June 2018).

38 These comments were made during the application of NZME and Fairfax to merge in 2016. The two groups' submission estimated that Google took 37.3 per cent of the New Zealand digital advertising market, while Facebook took 16.4 per cent: Fairfax New Zealand Ltd and Wilson & Horton Ltd, 'Notice seeking authorisation or clearance of a business acquisition', letter to the Commerce Commission, 27 May 2016, p.3, https://comcom.govt.nz/__data/assets/pdf_file/0035/77498/Fairfax-NZ-Ltd-and-Wilson-Horton-Ltd-Authorisation-application-27-May-2016-amended-24-August-2016.PDF (accessed 20 January 2019).

39 John Reinan, 'How Craigslist killed the newspapers' golden goose', *Minnpost*, 3 February 2014, www.minnpost.com/business/2014/02/how-craigslist-killed-newspapers-golden-goose (accessed 10 June 2018).

40 Jack Shafer and Tucker Doherty, 'The media bubble is

worse than you think', *Politico Magazine*, May/June 2017, www.politico.com/magazine/story/2017/04/25/media-bubble-real-journalism-jobs-east-coast-215048 (accessed 17 January 2019).

41 In 2019, the US media reportedly faced its worst job losses in a decade, with about 3,000 people laid off or offered redundancy in the first five months of the year. Gerry Smith, 'Journalism job cuts haven't been this bad since the recession', *Bloomberg*, 1 July 2019, www.bloomberg.com/news/articles/2019-07-01/journalism-layoffs-are-at-the-highest-level-since-last-recession (accessed 30 July 2019).

42 Alan Rusbridger, *Breaking News: The Remaking of Journalism and Why It Matters Now*, Canongate, London, 2018, p.74.

43 Penny Abernathy, *The Rise of a New Media Baron and the Emerging Threat of News Deserts*, Centre for Innovation and Sustainability in Local Media, University of North Carolina at Chapel Hill, 2016; and Penny Abernathy, *The Expanding News Desert*, Centre for Innovation and Sustainability in Local Media, University of North Carolina at Chapel Hill, 2018. See also Michelle Ferrier, Gaurav Sinha and Michael Outrich, 'Media deserts: Monitoring the changing media ecosystem', in M. Lloyd and L.A. Friedland (eds), *The Communication Crisis in America, and How to Fix It*, Palgrave Macmillan, New York, NY, 2016, pp.215–32.

44 Margaret Sullivan, '"Democracy … is about to die in Youngstown" with closing of the local newspaper', *Washington Post*, 7 July 2019, www.washingtonpost.com/lifestyle/style/democracy--is-about-to-die-in-youngstown-with-closing-of-the-local-newspaper/2019/07/05/e428e26a-9da4-11e9-b27f-ed2942f73d70_story.html?utm_term=.d5a31870b5c8 (accessed 30 July 2019).

45 James T. Hamilton and Fiona Morgan, 'Poor information: How economics affects the information lives of low-income individuals', *International Journal of Communication*, 12 (2018), pp.2832–50, https://ijoc.org/index.php/ijoc/article/viewFile/8340/2399 (accessed 19 July 2019).

46 Steven Waldman, *The Information Needs of Communities: The Changing Media Landscape in a Broadband Age*, Federal Communications Commission, July 2011, https://transition.fcc.gov/osp/inc-report/The_Information_Needs_of_Communities.pdf (accessed 20 January 2019).

47 'Charlottesville: Race and terror', *VICE News Tonight*, HBO, 14 August 2017, https://youtu.be/P54sP0Nlngg (accessed 26 July 2019).

48 Elizabeth Grieco, 'U.S. newsroom employment has dropped by a quarter since 2008, with greatest decline at newspapers', Pew Research Center, 9 July 2019, https://pewrsr.ch/2NHLbnP (accessed 19 July 2019).

49 Erin McKenzie, 'Public relations vs journalism: Is the rise of PR a threat to the fourth estate?', *StopPress*, 1 December 2015, http://stoppress.co.nz/news/public-service-journalism-versus-public-relations-professionals-uprising-pr-threatening-fourth-estate (accessed 9 June 2018).

50 *The Spinoff* describes itself as '[a] New Zealand site covering pop culture, politics and social life through features, criticism, interviews, videos and podcasts'. This emphasis on features, rather than news, is reflected in the categories it won in the 2018 Voyager Media Awards: essay, opinion, reviewing, features and artwork. In the 2019 awards, the outlet won best website, among other prizes.

51 Email from Toby Manhire, 29 July 2019.

52 Shafer and Doherty, 'The media bubble is worse than you think'. See also Ross Barkan, 'The biggest threat to journalism isn't Donald Trump. It's declining revenues', *Guardian*, 17 July 2017, www.theguardian.com/commentisfree/2017/jul/17/news-industry-revenue-declines-biggest-threat-to-journalism (accessed 8 January 2019); Shawn Musgrave and Matthew Nussbaum, 'Trump thrives in areas that lack traditional news outlets', *Politico*, 8 April 2018, www.politico.com/story/2018/04/08/news-subscriptions-decline-donald-trump-voters-505605 (accessed 9 June 2018).

53 The outlet is owned as a trust and supported by philanthropists, including

Dick Hubbard. The trust is also supported by the University of Canterbury's School of Journalism, which hopes it will help train and develop new journalists. The founders are optimistic about what can be done to support journalism moving forward, according to Colin Peacock: 'We're seeing the beginning of a New Zealand universe of new media. How exciting would it be to see New Zealand-owned media work in the regions and the metropolitan areas? *Newsroom, The Spinoff*, the Nelson and Wanaka apps are all part of the solution and I think we will all end up sharing and forming networks.' Colin Peacock, 'Boosting local journalism for the Southern Lakes', Radio New Zealand, 6 May 2018, www.rnz.co.nz/national/programmes/mediawatch/audio/2018643329/boosting-local-journalism-for-the-southern-lakes (accessed 19 January 2019).

54 In 2014, a UK survey of 183 hyperlocal sites found that 75 per cent had posted about local businesses in the last two years, 79 per cent had covered local government planning issues, and 81 per cent had covered local council meetings. Carina Tenor, 'Hyperlocal news: After the hype', POLIS report, London School of Economics, July 2018, p.1, www.lse.ac.uk/media-and-communications/assets/documents/research/Polis-Hyperlocal-News-report-Jul-2018.pdf (accessed 8 January 2019).

55 One UK survey found that only one in four were able to raise money to cover costs: the rest are doing it out of their own time and pocket. Andy Williams, Steven Barnett, Dave Harte and Judith Townend, 'The state of hyperlocal community news in the UK: Findings from a survey of practitioners', report based on a collaboration between the Media, Community and the Creative Citizen project, Cardiff and Birmingham City Universities, and the Media Power and Plurality project, based at the University of Westminster, July 2014, https://orca.cf.ac.uk/68425/1/hyperlocal-community-news-in-the-uk-2014.pdf (accessed 8 January 2018).

56 Steven Barnett and Judith Townend, 'Plurality, policy and the local: Can hyperlocals fill the gap?', *Journalism Practice*,

9, 3 (2015), pp.332–49, https://doi.org/10.1080/17512786.2014.943930 (accessed 19 July 2019).

57 Tenor, 'Hyperlocal news', p.10.

58 Andy Williams, Dave Harte and Jerome Turner, 'The value of UK hyperlocal community news', *Digital Journalism*, 3, 5 (2015), pp. 680–703, https://doi.org/10.1080/21670811.2014.965932 (accessed 19 July 2019). See also David Harte, Rachel Howells and Andy Williams, *Hyperlocal Journalism: The Decline of Local Newspapers and the Rise of Online Community News*, Routledge, London and New York, NY, 2018.

59 Cited in Tenor, 'Hyperlocal news', p.9.

60 Williams, Harte and Turner, 'The value of UK hyperlocal community news', p.691. This raises concerns about a lack of transparency, a lack of plurality in the sources of information to which audiences are exposed, and a lack of opportunity for audiences to learn about conflicting perspectives on particular issues. See also Harte, Howells and Williams, *Hyperlocal Journalism*.

61 Tenor, 'Hyperlocal news', p.12. Or as Andy Williams puts it in the same report: 'I think the hyperlocal sector should be celebrated for what it is, and not denigrated for what it is not.' It is also worth noting that the hyperlocals that have succeeded tend to be in areas where there are more people with enough money; and that is not always where journalism is needed the most.

62 Frederick Fico et al., 'Citizen journalism sites as information substitutes and complements for United States newspaper coverage of local governments', *Digital Journalism*, 1, 1 (2013), pp.152–68, https://doi.org/10.1080/21670811.2012.740270 (accessed 20 July 2019); K. Holt and M. Karlsson, '"Random acts of journalism?": How citizen journalists tell the news in Sweden', *New Media & Society*, 17, 11 (2014), pp.1795–810.

63 Clay Shirky, 'Newspapers and thinking the unthinkable', 13 March 2009, www.shirky.com/weblog/2009/03/newspapers-and-thinking-the-unthinkable (accessed 21 January 2019).

64 The *New York Times* now has more than 4 million paying readers. It has gone from 1,100 journalists in 2014 up to 1,500 in 2018: a 36 per cent rise in just four

years. In 2017, the paper made a billion dollars from subscriptions. The *Washington Post* is also growing. It does not post official numbers but an internal memo revealed digital-only subscribers had reached more than 1 million, doubling in a year. In 2018, it had 825 editorial employees – up from only 600 in 2016. Ken Doctor, 'Newsonomics: 18 lessons for the news business from 2018', Nieman Lab, 19 December 2018, www.niemanlab.org/2018/12/newsonomics-18-lessons-for-the-news-business-from-2018 (accessed 29 December 2018). It's worth noting that, for all that the *New York Times* is flourishing, it would still be in trouble if it was not for its crosswords and recipes. The outlet has 400,000 people who subscribe for this content alone, bringing in much needed money that is used to subsidise journalism. Other successful outlets are also 'cross funding' their journalism with related products and services. In the UK, the *Financial Times* brings in substantial revenue by running corporate events, while the *Guardian* has a range of additional events and products for readers, ranging from talks and workshops to an online dating service.

65 As Clay Shirky puts it, 'their stock tips are inside the pay wall, because people will pay for the fact that there's barriers. It's the $17 martini logic, right? What goes into a $17 martini is three dollars worth of gin and fourteen dollars worth of "I'm drinking in a place where people are drinking seventeen dollar martinis".' Joshua Benton, 'Clay Shirky: Let a thousand flowers bloom to replace newspapers; don't build a paywall around a public good', Nieman Lab, 23 September 2009, www.niemanlab.org/2009/09/clay-shirky-let-a-thousand-flowers-bloom-to-replace-newspapers-dont-build-a-paywall-around-a-public-good (accessed 20 July 2019).

66 Nic Newman et al., *Reuters Institute Digital News Report 2019*, Reuters Institute, Oxford, 2019, https://reutersinstitute.politics.ox.ac.uk/sites/default/files/2019-06/DNR_2019_FINAL_1.pdf (accessed 29 July 2019).

67 Jim Waterson, '"Just use cat videos": New York Times boss

wants Facebook to cut out news', *Guardian*, 3 August 2018, www.theguardian.com/media/2018/aug/03/just-use-cat-videos-new-york-times-boss-mark-thompson-wants-facebook-to-cut-out-news?CMP=Share_iOSApp_Other (accessed 21 January 2019).

68 Newman et al., *Reuters Institute Digital News Report 2019*.

69 Richard Fletcher and Rasmus Kleis Nielsen, 'Paying for online news: A comparative analysis of six countries', *Digital Journalism*, 5, 9 (2017), pp.1173–91, https://doi.org/10.1080/21670811.2016.1246373 (accessed 20 July 2019).

70 Eileen Culloty, 'Do the public have a responsibility to pay for online news?', *Irish Times*, 22 June 2017, www.irishtimes.com/opinion/do-the-public-have-a-responsibility-to-pay-for-online-news-1.3129447 (accessed 9 June 2018).

71 As Alan Rusbridger commented of the UK media market, even in the absolute pits of despair in the newspaper crisis there has 'never been a shortage of billionaires and oligarchies to keep the show on the row',

Rusbridger, *Breaking News*, p.167.

72 Rory Carroll, 'Interview: The billionaire who bought the LA Times: "Hipsters will want paper soon"', *Guardian*, 21 July 2018, www.theguardian.com/media/2018/jul/21/los-angeles-times-new-owner-patrick-soon-shiong-interview (accessed 20 July 2019).

73 Ibid.

74 Rusbridger, *Breaking News*, p.338.

75 Mathew Ingram, 'Facebook says it plans to put $300M into journalism projects', *Columbia Journalism Review*, 15 January 2019, www.cjr.org/the_new_gatekeepers/facebook-journalism-funding.php (accessed 15 January 2019).

76 See Mathew Ingram, 'The platform patrons: How Facebook and Google became two of the biggest funders of journalism in the world', *Columbia Journalism Review*, 16 May 2018, www.cjr.org/special_report/google-facebook-journalism.php (accessed 15 January 2019).

77 Merja Myllylahti, *Google, Facebook and New Zealand News Media: The Problem of Platform Dependency*, report prepared for The

Policy Observatory, AUT, September 2018, p.13, https://thepolicyobservatory.aut.ac.nz/__data/assets/pdf_file/0017/202841/google-facebook-and-new-zealand-news-media-merja-myllylahti.pdf (accessed 20 July 2019).

78 Elizabeth Green, 'What I wish everyone who cared about local news knew about local news', *Medium*, 26 September 2018, https://medium.com/trust-media-and-democracy/what-i-wish-everyone-who-cared-about-local-news-knew-about-local-news-acbdd544469a (accessed 20 January 2018).

79 The director of Amedia also notes that Google did not affect newspapers in Norway the same way it did in other countries, because the search engine primarily operates in English. Em Kuntze, 'How do you succeed with subscriptions? We asked Amedia's Pål Nedregotten', Content Insights, 17 May 2017, https://contentinsights.com/how-do-you-succeed-with-subscriptions (accessed 4 August 2019).

80 'The Texas Tribune's secret sauce, with Emily Ramshaw', podcast 'Recode Media with Peter Kafka', 3 July 2019, www.stitcher.com/podcast/vox/recode-media-with-peter-kafka/e/62352954 (accessed 5 August 2019).

Chapter 2

1 Joseph Schumpeter and Robert Dahl argue that a representative democracy has three main structural features: (1) *pluralistic competition* among parties and individuals for government positions; (2) *participation* by citizens in the selection of parties and representatives through free, fair and periodic elections, and 3) *civil and political liberties* to speak, publish, assemble, and organise, the final one being necessary to ensure effective competition and participation. Norris argues that the news media plays a crucial role in ensuring these criteria are satisfied, doing work that no other institutions or organisations can. Norris notes there are other criteria we could use to evaluate the media – for example, the extent to which it helps to achieve educational or cultural goals. But these are not its core political functions in a representative democracy. It is also worth noting that 'representative democracy' is only one of many approaches.

Others argue for a more direct or participatory system of democracy. However, the Schumpeterian perspective is arguably the most widely accepted. And, as it is a 'thin' definition, it offers a good starting point for discussing the *minimum* requirements of the news media in a democracy. That is, one that people from different ends of the political spectrum could agree was required. See Pippa Norris, *A Virtuous Circle: Political Communications in Postindustrial Societies*, Cambridge University Press, Cambridge, 2000, pp.22–32.

2   Social theorists have written extensively about the need for trustworthy information within a democracy, and the unique position of journalists to provide this. See Herbert Gans, *Democracy and the News*, Oxford University Press, Oxford, 2003; John Keane, *The Media and Democracy*, Polity Press, Cambridge, 1991; James Curran, 'Mediations of democracy', in J. Curran and M. Gurevitch (eds), *Mass Media and Society*, 4th edn, Hodder Arnold, London, 2005, pp.122–49; Peter J. Anderson and Geoff Ward (eds), *The Future of Journalism in the Advanced Democracies*, Ashgate, Aldershot, 2007; David Levy and Rasmus Kleis Nielsen (eds), *The Changing Business of Journalism and Its Implications for Democracy*, Reuters Institute, Oxford, 2010.

3   Rachel Howells, 'Journey to the centre of a news black hole: Examining the democratic deficit in a town with no newspaper', PhD thesis, School of Journalism, Media and Cultural Studies, University of Cardiff, 2015, p.249.

4   Rasmus Kleis Nielsen, 'Introduction: The uncertain future of local journalism', in Rasmus Kleis Nielsen (ed.), *Local Journalism: The Decline of Newspapers and the Rise of Digital Media*, I. B. Tauris & Co. Ltd in association with the Reuters Institute, Oxford, 2015, p.16. See also Yong-Chan Kim and Sandra J. Ball-Rokeach, 'Community storytelling network, neighborhood context, and civic engagement: A multilevel approach', *Human Communication Research*, 32, 4 (2006), pp.411–39, https://doi.org/10.1111/j.1468-2958.2006.00282.x (accessed 19 July 2019); Morris

Janowitz, *The Community Press in an Urban Setting*, Free Press, Glencoe, IL, 1952; and Rod Kirkpatrick, 'The mirror of local life: Country newspapers, country values and country content', in Perry Share (ed.), *Communication and Culture in Rural Areas*, Centre for Rural Social Research, Wagga Wagga, 1995, pp.219–38.

5   Benedict Anderson, *Imagined Communities: Reflections on the Origin and Spread of Nationalism*, Verso, London, 1983. It is important to note that the 'imagined community' of the state can be a very exclusionary form of nationalism, as many scholars have pointed out: see, for example, Partha Chatterjee, 'Whose imagined community', *Millennium: Journal of International Studies*, 20, 3 (1991), pp.521–25.

6   One important longitudinal study compared more than 10,000 news articles with voting rates, and showed that, as local coverage of politics shrank in US communities, so too did voter turnout. Danny Hayes and Jennifer L. Lawless, 'The decline of local news and its effects: New evidence from longitudinal data', *Journal of Politics*, 80, 1 (2018), pp.332–36, http://dx.doi.org/10.1086/694105 (accessed 19 July 2019). This is the case even when researchers control for socio-economic variables and the levels of political interest among citizens. See Dietram A. Scheufele, James Shanahan and Sei-Hill Kim, 'Who cares about local politics? Media influences on local political involvement, issue awareness, and attitude strength', *Journalism and Mass Communication Quarterly*, 79, 2 (2002), pp.427–44; Lee Shaker, 'Dead newspapers and citizens' civic engagement', *Political Communication*, 31, 1 (2014), pp.131–48, https://doi.org/10.1080/1058460 9.2012.762817 (accessed 19 July 2019); Matthew Gentzkow, Jesse M. Shapiro and Michael Sinkinson, 'The effect of newspaper entry and exit on electoral politics', NBER Working Paper 15544, 2009, www.nber.org/papers/w15544; Martin Baekgaard, Carsten Jensen, Peter B. Mortensen and Søren Serritzlew, 'Local news media and voter turnout', *Local Government Studies*, 40, 4 (2014), pp.518–32, https://

doi.org/10.1080/03003930.2 013.834253 (accessed 19 July 2019); Jackie Filla and Martin Johnson, 'Local news outlets and political participation', *Urban Affairs Review*, 45, 5 (2010), pp.679–92; Sam Schulhofer-Wohl and Miguel Garrido, 'Do newspapers matter? Short-run and long-run evidence from the closure of The Cincinnati Post', *Journal of Media Economics*, 26, 2 (2013), pp.60–81.

7   These issues are explored in a book that I coedited with Suzanne Franks and Chris Paterson: *Africa's Media Image in the 21st Century: From the 'Heart of Darkness' to 'Africa Rising'*, Routledge, Abingdon, 2016.

8   James Ferguson, *Global Shadows: Africa in the Neoliberal World Order*, Duke University Press, London, 2006. This has direct and important implications for trade, tourism and intercultural relations. See also Achille Mbembe, *On the Postcolony*, University of California Press, London, 2001.

9   Mike Pflanz, 'Become a Facebook friend with a mountain gorilla', *Telegraph*, 2 September 2009, www.

telegraph.co.uk/technology/ facebook/6123365/Become-a-Facebook-friend-with-a-mountain-gorilla.html (accessed 15 January 2019).

10   Henrik Örnebring and Anna Maria Jönsson, 'Tabloid journalism and the public sphere: A historical perspective on tabloid journalism', *Journalism Studies*, 5, 3 (2004), pp.283–95, https://doi. org/10.1080/1461670042 000246052 (accessed 19 July 2019).

11   Pulitzer, who was an immigrant, often railed against the conditions in which many of New York's immigrant labourers lived. In July 1883, a heat wave caused the deaths of over 700 in the slums – over half of them children under the age of five – and Pulitzer used sensational headlines and shocking narrative to try to force the City authorities to address the housing issues. For a wider discussion, see Edwin Emery and Michael Emery, *The Press and America: An Interpretive History of the Mass Media,* Prentice Hall, Englewood Cliffs, NJ, 1978.

12   Less happily, this legislation also recriminalised homosexual acts in the UK.

13 See Michael Schudson, *The Power of News*, Harvard University Press, Cambridge, MA, 1995, p.76.

14 The show *Last Week Tonight with John Oliver* in the US is a good example of this. John Oliver has a team of researchers that fact check the claims in his show. Because of the format, and huge audience, he's able to raise issues in a way that few others are. See, for example, Rick Edmonds, 'I was interviewed by "Last Week Tonight." Here's why the show is journalism', *Poynter*, 8 August 2016, www.poynter.org/newsletters/2016/i-was-interviewed-by-last-week-tonight-heres-why-the-show-is-journalism (accessed 21 January 2019).

15 See Paul Leicester Ford (ed.), *The Works of Thomas Jefferson*, Federal Edition, G. P. Putnam's Sons, New York and London, Volume 5, 1904–5, http://oll.libertyfund.org/titles/jefferson-the-works-vol-5-correspondence-1786-1789 (accessed 8 June 2018). This volume contains various letters and papers from the years 1786–89.

16 James W. Carey, 'Journalism and democracy are names for the same thing', Nieman Reports, 15 June 2000, https://niemanreports.org/articles/journalism-and-democracy-are-names-for-the-same-thing (accessed 19 July 2019).

17 Tim Snyder, *On Tyranny: Twenty Lessons from the Twentieth Century*, Bodley Head, London, 2017.

18 David Harte, Rachel Howells and Andy Williams (eds), *Hyperlocal Journalism: The Decline of Local Newspapers and the Rise of Online Community News*, Routledge, London, 2018, pp.11–12; Dawn Foster, 'People died thinking "they didn't listen", says ex-Grenfell residents' group chair', *Guardian*, 15 June 2017, www.theguardian.com/uk-news/2017/jun/15/former-grenfell-tower-resident-demands-independent-inquiry-into-fire (accessed 8 June 2018).

19 Grant Feller worked as a journalist on local papers in Kensington, London (the site of Grenfell) in the 1990s. His newspaper had ten full-time journalists, and competed with another in the borough. Feller believes that the story would absolutely have been reported when he was working: 'Any local newspaper journalist worth his or her salt would

have been all over that story because of that blog. … We would have poured [sic] over the council meeting agendas and asked questions of the councillors and the officers.' Today, however, there is only one journalist working in the borough and '[t]hose people can do what they like because there's [sic] no journalists looking at what they are doing'. Dominic Ponsford, 'Former Kensington reporter says local press would have picked up on Grenfell fire-safety concerns in pre-internet era', *PressGazette*, 22 June 2017, www.pressgazette.co.uk/ former-kensington-reporter-says-local-press-would-have-picked-up-on-grenfell-fire-safety-concerns-in-pre-internet-era (accessed 25 November 2018).

20 Ethan Zuckerman, 'Four problems for news and democracy', *Medium*, 2 April 2018, https://medium.com/ trust-media-and-democracy/ we-know-the-news-is-in-crisis-5d1c4fbf7691 (accessed 13 June 2018). Michael Schudson, a media sociologist and historian at Columbia University, makes a similar argument, noting that '[j]ournalism can perform its institutional role as a watchdog even if nobody in the provinces is following the news. All that matters is that people in government *believe* they are following the news. If an inner circle of attentive citizens is watchful, this is sufficient to produce in the leaders a fear of public embarrassment, public controversy, legal prosecution, or fear of losing an election. The job of the media, in this respect, is to make powerful people tremble.' Michael Schudson, 'News in crisis in the United States: Panic – and beyond', in Levy and Nielsen (eds), *The Changing Business of Journalism and Its Implications for Democracy*, p.103. Rasmus Nielsen makes a similar point in his book *Local Journalism* (p.67): 'We know from years of research that the very fact that news is made public – even when its audience is limited – helps keep local government and local politicians responsive to their constituents, this news production is important for the local political information environment and for local democracy even when few read it and no one else follows up on it.'

21 James T. Hamilton, *Democracy's Detectives: The Economics of Investigative Journalism*, Harvard University Press, Cambridge, MA, 2016.

22 James Hollings, 'Matt Nippert and the beautiful possibilities of investigative journalism', *The Spinoff*, 7 August 2017, https://thespinoff.co.nz/books/07-08-2017/matt-nippert-and-the-beautiful-possibilities-of-investigative-journalism (accessed 20 May 2018).

23 BBC, 'New Zealand intelligence failed on fantasist scientist', BBC News, 28 January 2011, www.bbc.com/news/world-asia-pacific-12304651 (accessed 19 August 2018).

24 The inquiry can be read at New Zealand Defence Force, 'Court of Inquiry into the Circumstances in which Mr Stephen Wilce was employed as Director of the Defence Technology Agency', NZDF 5202-2 S. Wilce – DTA, revised 2009, www.nzdf.mil.nz/downloads/pdf/public-docs/2010/nzdf-coi-wilce-report.pdf (accessed 19 August 2018).

25 Of course, many factors may influence the behaviour of gas and oil companies – and some of these factors might also be linked to the presence of a newspaper (for example, education levels, population density or civic engagement). Campa controlled for these variables by analysing whether the presence of a university had the same impact (because, like newspapers, universities are concentrated in areas where people are more informed and more likely to vote). She found the presence of a university did not have the same impact as the presence of a news outlet. Pamela Campa, 'Press and leaks: Do newspapers reduce toxic emissions?', *Journal of Environmental Economics and Management*, 91, C (September 2018), pp.184–202, https://econpapers.repec.org/RePEc:eee:jeeman:v:91:y:2018:i:c:p:184-202 (accessed 19 July 2019).

26 Jürgen Habermas (trans. Thomas Burger), *The Structural Transformation of the Public Sphere: An Inquiry into a Category of Bourgeois Society*, Polity Press, Cambridge, 1989. For further discussion, see William Outhwaite, *Habermas: A Critical Introduction*, Polity Press, Cambridge, 1994.

27 Former Prime Minister Sir Geoffrey Palmer gives the example of an 1850 'great public meeting' in Nelson, where citizens debated how New Zealand should be governed. A detailed account was published in the *Nelson Examiner*, with a memorandum directly addressed to Governor Grey. This type of reporting captured the mood and views of citizens, and articulated them to fellow citizens, as well as the elites and decision-makers in Great Britain, informing their approach to governance. Palmer concludes: 'Free people trying to achieve a measure of self-government needed to have a newspaper.' See Geoffrey Palmer, 'The strong New Zealand democratic tradition and the "Great Public Meeting" of 1850 in Nelson', *New Zealand Journal of Public and International Law*, 12, 1 (2014), pp.205–30, www.victoria.ac.nz/law/centres/nzcpl/publications/nz-journal-of-public-and-international-law/previous-issues/volume-121,-september-2014/Palmer.pdf (accessed 19 July 2019). See also Ian F. Grant, *Lasting Impressions: The Story of New Zealand Newspapers, 1840–1920*, Fraser Books in association with the Alexander Turnbull Library, Wellington, 2018.

28 Matthew Nickless, 'Through the red lens: Constructed perceptions of Māori as a violent race, 1857–1873', Master's thesis, University of Auckland, 2017.

29 The famous idea of the 'CNN effect' was coined after blanket, 24/7 coverage of the Somalia famine of 1991–92 on cable TV appeared to prompt President Bush Snr to intervene in the crisis. This rather simplistic interpretation was challenged by subsequent research, which actually showed the opposite: news coverage *followed* the President's decision to act. Toward the end of the 1990s, researchers took a more balanced line, suggesting that extensive news coverage can *sometimes* influence governments' foreign or aid policies when political objectives and strategies had not already been clearly defined. See Steven Livingston, 'Clarifying the CNN effect: An examination of media effects according to type of military intervention', Research Paper R-18, The Shorenstein Center on Media, Politics and Public

Policy, John F. Kennedy School of Government, Harvard University, Cambridge, MA, June 1997.

30 Shanto Iyengar and Donald R. Kinder, *News that Matters: Television and American Opinion*, University of Chicago Press, Chicago, IL, 1987.

31 The researchers suggest this may be explained by the fact that, without local news, citizens rely more on national media as a source, which is – as a general rule – more focused on political parties and partisanship differences. Local media outlets, by contrast, are more likely to assess the policy and candidates on pragmatic terms. They are also more likely to offer a centrist position, as they cater their content to audiences with a wide range of political views. Joshua P. Darr, Matthew P. Hitt and Johanna L. Dunaway, 'Newspaper closures polarize voting behavior', *Journal of Communication*, 68, 6 (2018), pp.1007–28, https://doi.org/10.1093/joc/jqy051 (accessed 19 July 2019).

32 Richard Mulgan, *Politics in New Zealand*, 3rd edn, Auckland University Press, 2004, p.289.

33 In the 1990s and 2000s, numerous studies documented the news media's negative portrayal of gay people and issues. Gays and lesbians were routinely presented as criminals, mentally ill, sexual perverts, and/or radical militants posing a threat to the social order. They were also constructed as victims of abuse and disease, trapped against their will in an immoral lifestyle. See, for example, Edward Alwood, *Straight News: Gay Men, Lesbians, and the News Media*, Columbia University Press, New York, NY, 1996; L. Bennett, 'Fifty years of prejudice in the media', *The Gay and Lesbian Review*, 7, 2 (2000), pp.30–35; Larry Gross, *Up from Invisibility: Lesbians, Gay Men, and the Media in America*, Columbia University Press, New York, NY, 2001; and Richard A. McKay, *Patient Zero and the Making of the AIDS Epidemic*, Chicago University Press, Chicago, IL, 2017. These representations improved dramatically through the late 2000s and 2010s, although gay issues are still sometimes presented as deviant, and gay voices are frequently silenced within debate. See, for example, Leigh

M. Moscowitz, 'Gay marriage in television news: Voice and visual representation in the same-sex marriage debate', *Journal of Broadcasting & Electronic Media*, 54, 1 (2010), pp.24–39, https://doi.org/10.1080/0883815090 3550360 (accessed 19 July 2019).

34 A wealth of research has focused on the stigmatisation of specific health conditions, and mental health-related issues in particular, including obesity, anorexia nervosa, HIV/AIDS and schizophrenia: see Gary Morris, *Mental Health Issues and the Media: An Introduction for Health Professionals*, Routledge, New York, NY, 2006. In their content analysis of coverage of mental illness in US newspapers in 2005, Corrigan et al. found an emphasis on blame, treatment, recovery and calls to action. The study also indicated mental illnesses were stigmatised as dangerous, suicidal and threatening to the public. P.W. Corrigan et al., 'Newspaper stories as measures of structural stigma', *Psychiatric Services*, 56, 5 (2005), pp.551–56, https://doi.org/10.1176/appi.ps.56.5.551 (accessed 19 July 2019). Negativity and generic labelling were found in a similar study of New Zealand newspapers. J. Coverdale, R. Nairn and D. Classen, 'Depictions of mental illness in print media: A prospective national sample', *Australian and New Zealand Journal of Psychiatry*, 36, 5 (2002), pp.697–700, https://doi.org/10.1046/j.1440-1614.2002.00998.x (accessed 19 July 2019).

35 Bunce, Franks and Paterson (eds), *Africa's Media Image in the 21st Century*.

36 Iyengar and Kinder, *News that Matters*.

Chapter 3

1 Roy Greenslade, 'Why New Zealand's journalists should push for a new form of ownership', *Guardian*, 7 December 2016, www.theguardian.com/media/greenslade/2016/dec/07/why-new-zealands-journalists-should-push-for-a-new-form-of-ownership (accessed 31 May 2017).

2 As James T. Hamilton, an economist and Director of the Journalism Program at Stanford University, explains: 'The resources devoted to researching a story, composing its presentation, and making

the first copy for delivery can be tremendous. They may involve fixed costs of maintaining a set of reporters and a configuration of costly production and transmission technology. The second or subsequent copies of a news good may involve relatively small costs, such as print or paper for daily newspapers or server space for Internet sites. The high size of fixed costs limits the number of providers who can survive in a particular news market.' James T. Hamilton, 'News that sells: Media competition and news content', *Japanese Journal of Political Science*, 8, 1 (2007), pp.7–42, https://doi.org/10.1017/S1468109907002460 (accessed 20 July 2019).

3   One consequence of this is that we bring a lot of recycled material in from overseas, which is a cheaper way to fill the airwaves and newspapers. The proportion of local content on TV, in particular, is very low, owing to the high costs of making original content. In 2016, only 31 per cent of programming during prime-time TV was locally made – down from 43.3 per cent a decade earlier. Office of

the Minister of Broadcasting, Communications and Digital Media, 'Ministerial Advisory Group: Allocation of funding and role of a public media funding commission', Cabinet Paper, 2018, p.3, www.beehive.govt.nz/sites/default/files/2018-02/Cabinet%20Paper%20on%20the%20Advisory%20Group%20for%20the%20Public%20Media%20Funding%20Commission%20redacted.pdf (accessed 20 July 2019).

4   AKA Shark Week.

5   James Hollings, Folker Hanusch, Geoff Lealand and Ravi Balasubramanian, 'Country report: Journalists in New Zealand', *Worlds of Journalism Study*, 22 December 2016, https://epub.ub.uni-muenchen.de/32088/1/Country_report_New_Zealand.pdf (accessed 12 March 2018); Kevin Rafter, Lydia Frost and Thomas Hanitzsch, 'Country report: Journalists in Ireland', *Worlds of Journalism Study*, 2 March 2017, https://epub.ub.uni-muenchen.de/35065/1/Country_report_Ireland.pdf (accessed 12 March 2018).

6   Thomas Owen, 'Neocolonialism, nation-building and global journalism

in Aotearoa news', in Emma Johnson, Giovanni Tiso, Sarah Illingworth and Barnaby Bennett (eds), *Don't Dream It's Over: Reimagining Journalism in Aotearoa New Zealand*, Freerange Press, Christchurch, 2016, p.106.

7   Merja Myllylahti, *New Zealand Media Ownership 2016*, AUT Research Centre for Journalism, Media and Democracy, December 2016, www.aut.ac.nz/__data/assets/pdf_file/0020/107057/JMAD-Report-2016.pdf (accessed 20 July 2019).

8   Merja Myllylahti, *New Zealand Media Ownership 2018*, AUT Research Centre for Journalism, Media and Democracy, December 2018, www.aut.ac.nz/__data/assets/pdf_file/0013/231511/JMAD-2018-Report.pdf (accessed 21 January 2019).

9   Bertelsmann Stiftung Foundation, 'Quality of Democracy: Access to Information', www.sgi-network.org/2016/Democracy/Quality_of_Democracy/Access_to_Information/Media_Pluralism (accessed 27 December 2018).

10 Myllylahti, *New Zealand Media Ownership 2018*, p.53.

11 Up until the 1980s, almost all newspapers in New Zealand were owned by local families and companies. Derby, 'Newspapers'.

12 This does not mean they will necessarily make 'bad journalism'. It is possible to make profit selling quality journalism, as, for example, the *Economist* does. However, this usually involves having access to a very large market.

13 Penny Abernathy, *The Rise of a New Media Baron and the Emerging Threat of News Deserts*, Centre for Innovation and Sustainability in Local Media, University of North Carolina at Chapel Hill, 2016, p.7. There are a handful of exceptions. But for the general, commercial media, without a vested interest in the community they serve, there is an ongoing temptation to cut costs or change the product to increase revenue.

14 Alan Freeman, 'Canada plans hefty aid package for its struggling media sector. Not everyone is pleased', *Washington Post*, 28 November 2018, www.washingtonpost.com/world/2018/11/28/canada-plans-hefty-aid-package-its-struggling-media-sector-not-everyone-is-

pleased/?noredirect=
on&utm_term=.79d02af91e09
(accessed 20 July 2019).

15 Another prominent example
is Alden Global Capital in
the US, which owns sixty
daily newspapers through
a subsidiary, Digital First
Media, and has been singled
out for particular criticism
after making savage cuts. One
of the group's newspapers,
the *Denver Post*, was forced
to cut its editorial staff from
200 to fewer than 100 in an
eight-year period. In 2018,
the newspaper's remaining
employees published a
controversial editorial
warning that the management
strategy would result in the
Post becoming nothing but
'rotting bones'. Digital First
Media argues that these cuts
are necessary to ensure the
survival of journalism. But the
company also made profits
of almost US$160 million in
2017, and had a 17 per cent
operating margin – well
above those of its peers. Ken
Doctor, 'Newsonomics: Alden
Global Capital is making
so much money wrecking
local journalism it might not
want to stop anytime soon',
Nieman Lab, 1 May 2018,
www.niemanlab.org/2018/05/
newsonomics-alden-global-
capital-is-making-so-much-
money-wrecking-local-
journalism-it-might-not-
want-to-stop-anytime-soon
(accessed 20 July 2019).

16 Thomas Pfeiffer, 'Hedge fund
follows U.S. playbook with
U.K. newspapers takeover',
Bloomberg, 20 November 2018,
www.bloomberg.com/news/
articles/2018-11-19/hedge-
fund-follows-u-s-playbook-
with-u-k-newspapers-
takeover (accessed 20 July
2019).

17 As media analyst Ken Doctor
argues, when news owners
have a short-term orientation,
the only results will be
'managed decline … [u]nless
you've got really deep pockets
and philanthropic intentions,
then it's cut'. Ken Doctor,
'Newsonomics: 18 lessons for
the news business from 2018',
Nieman Lab, 19 December
2018, www.niemanlab.
org/2018/12/newsonomics-
18-lessons-for-the-news-
business-from-2018 (accessed
29 December 2018).

18 Quoted in Gerry Smith, 'The
hard truth at newspapers
across America: Hedge
funds are in charge',
Bloomberg, 22 May 2018,
www.bloomberg.com/news/

articles/2018-05-22/the-hard-truth-at-newspapers-across-america-hedge-funds-are-in-charge (accessed 10 January 2019).

19   Susan Edmunds and Tom Pullar-Strecker, 'Stuff to sell or close 28 community and rural newspapers', Stuff, 21 February 2018, www.stuff.co.nz/business/101632830/stuff-outlines-newspaper-closures-as-part-of-shift-to-digital (accessed 20 July 2019).

20   Interview with a New Zealand newspaper editor, May 2017. Many other commentators have made these comments publicly. Sir Julian Smith, owner of Allied Press, New Zealand's only remaining independent newspaper company, has expressed concern about the truncation of local reporting, and the staff being laid off. David Williams, 'MediaRoom: Papers, paywalls and public money', Newsroom, 18 September 2018, www.newsroom.co.nz/2018/09/17/241198/odt-owner-on-papers-paywalls-and-public-money (accessed 2 January 2018).

21   Chris Barton, 'Anatomy of a redundancy: The suffocation of long-form journalism in New Zealand', in Johnson, Tiso, Illingworth and Bennett (eds), Don't Dream It's Over, pp.145–46.

22   In the lead-up to this decision, the Commission consulted international media experts David Levy, Senior Research Associate at Oxford University, and Robin Foster, media policy adviser and founder of the Communications Chambers consultancy. Levy and Foster compared the range of news sources available to New Zealanders with those available in countries of a similar size or geography – Finland, Denmark, Norway, Ireland and Australia. The assessment concluded that, compared with these others, 'the New Zealand news market is already more concentrated, there is relatively little routine use of news sources from outside New Zealand … [and] the level of public service provision in New Zealand is relatively low'. David Levy and Robin Foster, 'Impact of the proposed NZME/Fairfax merger on media plurality in New Zealand: Expert review of the Commerce Commission's Draft Determination Document', 16 November 2016, https://comcom.govt.nz/__data/assets/

pdf_file/0031/77575/Expert-report-on-Commissions-draft-determination-on-NZME-Fairfax-authorisation-16-November-2016.pdf (accessed 27 December 2018).

23 'Editors tell the Commerce Commission declining media merger is "wrong"', Stuff, 26 November 2016, www.stuff.co.nz/business/86782357/editors-tell-the-commerce-commission-declining-media-merger-is-wrong (accessed 20 July 2019).

24 The conflict between pro-merger and anti-merger groups often boiled down to two questions that, by their very nature, required guesswork: 1) What would happen in a counterfactual future where there was not a merger?; and 2) Did you believe the claims that the merged company would reinvest in journalism? As well as evidence, people made their guesses based on personal experience and opinion: did they know the people involved; did they work at a company with skin in the game; did they think the behaviour of other international investment groups that owned news groups was a good predictor of how these ones would behave? Even more generally, were they cynical or positive about human nature?

25 These figures were collected by Nordic on behalf of the Canadian Government review into public spending on media.

26 Quoted in an interview with Anders Hofseth, 'Emily Bell thinks public service media today has its most important role to play since World War II', Nieman Lab, 2 April 2018, www.niemanlab.org/2018/04/emily-bell-thinks-public-service-media-today-has-its-most-important-role-to-play-since-world-war-ii (accessed 27 December 2018).

27 Rodney Benson and Matthew Powers, 'Public media and political independence: Lessons for the future of journalism from around the world', public policy report, Free Press, Washington, DC, February 2011, p.45.

28 The implications of deregulation and competition on TV news is a very well-researched area of the New Zealand media. See Joe Atkinson, 'The state, the media and thin democracy', in Andrew Sharp (ed.), *Leap into the Dark: The Changing Role of the State in New Zealand since 1984*, Auckland

University Press, 1994, pp.146–77; Sarah Baker, 'The changing face of current affairs television programmes in New Zealand 1984–2004', PhD thesis, Auckland University of Technology, 2012; Margie Comrie, 'The commercial imperative in broadcasting news: TVNZ from 1985 to 1990', PhD thesis, Massey University, Palmerston North, 1996; Daniel Cook, 'Deregulation and broadcast news content: One network news from 1984 to 96', PhD thesis, University of Auckland, 2000.

29 Margie Comrie and Susan Fountaine, 'Retrieving public service broadcasting: Treading a fine line at TVNZ', *Media, Culture & Society*, 27, 1 (2005), pp.101–18, https://doi.org/10.1177%2F0163443705049060 (accessed 20 July 2019).

30 Peter Thompson, 'Unto God or unto Caesar? Television after the TVNZ charter', *Communication Journal of New Zealand*, 5, 2 (2004), pp.60–91, www.victoria.ac.nz/seftms/about/staff/peter-thompson/Unto-God-or-Unto-Caesar_CJNZ2004.pdf (accessed 20 July 2019).

31 This was similar to changes that happened in the US media market. There, the average sound bite in news coverage of presidential elections in 1972 was 25 seconds. By the 1988 election season, it was less than 9 seconds. Daniel C. Hallin, 'Sound bite news: Television coverage of elections, 1968–1988', *Journal of Communication*, 42, 2 (1992), pp.5–24, https://doi.org/10.1111/j.1460-2466.1992.tb00775.x (accessed 20 July 2019). A short soundbite is not necessarily a bad thing; short segments may be better critiqued and analysed within news programmes, whereas longer quotes can let politicians dominate the news and the framing of events without contestation. See also Megan Foley, 'Sound bites: Rethinking the circulation of speech from fragment to fetish', *Rhetoric and Public Affairs*, 15, 4 (2012), pp.613–22, www.jstor.org/stable/41940624 (accessed 20 July 2019).

32 Louisa Cleave, 'TVNZ welcomes $10m, wanted more', *New Zealand Herald*, 13 May 2002, www.nzherald.co.nz/nz/news/article.cfm?c_id=1&objectid=1844234 (accessed 9 June 2018).

33 Comrie and Fountaine,

'Retrieving public service broadcasting', p.115.

34 As Diana Wichtel put it in 2005, 'the time-honoured tradition of treating viewers like morons hasn't changed'. Diana Wichtel, 'Quite hard news', *New Zealand Listener*, 5 February 2005, www.noted.co.nz/archive/listener-nz-2005/quite-hard-news (accessed 9 June 2018).

35 Adam Dudding, 'Where now for TV current affairs?', Stuff, 4 June 2015, www.stuff.co.nz/entertainment/tv-radio/69031487/where-now-for-tv-current-affairs (accessed 10 June 2018).

36 Peter Thompson, 'Last chance to see? Public broadcasting policy and the public sphere in New Zealand', in Martin Hirst, Sean Phelan and Verica Rupar (eds), *Scooped: The Politics and Power of Journalism in Aotearoa New Zealand*, AUT Media, Auckland, 2012, p.106.

37 Former Broadcasting Minister Jonathan Coleman allegedly used the wrong ratings to prove the channel was failing. Its last viewership survey suggested that it was watched by more than half of all Freeview households. 'Stifled report doesn't save TVNZ7', *Newshub*, 25 November 2012.

38 'New Zealand Herald's first long-form documentary "Under the Bridge" out today', *New Zealand Herald*, 7 February 2017, www.nzherald.co.nz/nz/news/article.cfm?c_id=1&objectid=11793509 (accessed 20 July 2019).

39 Julia Cagé (trans. Arthur Goldhammer), *Saving the Media: Capitalism, Crowdfunding, and Democracy*, Harvard University Press, Cambridge, MA, 2016.

40 This partly reflects the fact that, seeking to fill their pages, it can be cheaper to take pre-existing content from newswires, international outlets and social media than to make original content.

41 Atkinson, 'The state, the media and thin democracy', p.152.

42 Baker, 'The changing face of current affairs television programmes in New Zealand 1984–2004', p.142.

43 Comrie and Fountaine, 'Retrieving public service broadcasting: Treading a fine line at TVNZ'.

44 Nadine Higgins, 'TVNZ criticising Netflix is like the old pot calling the kettle black', Stuff, 9 July 2017, www.stuff.co.nz/entertainment/tv-radio/94466546/nadine-higgins-poor-old-tvnz-its-on-

a-hiding-to-nothing (accessed 9 June 2018).

45 Rasmus Kleis Nielsen (ed.), *Local Journalism: The Decline of Newspapers and the Rise of Digital Media*, I. B. Tauris & Co. Ltd in association with the Reuters Institute, Oxford, 2015; Karin Wahl-Jorgensen, 'The challenge of local news provision', *Journalism*, 20, 1 (2019), pp.163–66, https://doi.org/10.1177%2F1464884918809281 (accessed 20 July 2019); Sam Ford with Christopher Ali, *The Future of Local News in New York City,* Tow Center for Digital Journalism, Columbia University, 2018, www1.nyc.gov/assets/mome/pdf/local-news-in-nyc.pdf (accessed 18 January 2019).

46 Wahl-Jorgensen, 'The challenge of local news provision'.

47 Robert G. Picard, 'Shifts in newspaper advertising expenditures and their implications for the future of newspapers', *Journalism Studies*, 9, 5 (2008), pp.704–16, https://doi.org/10.1080/14616700802207649 (accessed 20 July 2019).

48 Gordon Ramsay and Martin Moore, 'Monopolising local news: Is there an emerging local democratic deficit in the UK due to the decline of local newspapers?', Centre for the Study of Media, Communication and Power, King's College London, 2016, www.kcl.ac.uk/policy-institute/assets/cmcp/local-news.pdf (accessed 30 July 2019). It's very difficult to accurately measure declining print outlets and circulation, while taking into account the newspapers that have moved online. One good attempt in the UK has quantified the number of local newspapers/websites and their readership. In total, 271 of 406 Local Authority Districts in the UK (66.8 per cent) are not served by a dedicated local daily newspaper; 82 LADs are directly served; and 53 are covered by local dailies based in adjacent or nearby LADs.

49 Ford, *The Future of Local News in New York City*.

50 Paul Moses, 'In New York City, local coverage declines—and takes accountability with it', *The Daily Beast*, updated 5 May 2017, www.thedailybeast.com/in-new-york-city-local-coverage-declinesand-takes-accountability-with-it?ref=author (accessed 18 January 2019).

51 Rick Neville, 'New public media fund to boost regional news coverage', Stuff, 27 May 2019, www.stuff.co.nz/business/opinion-analysis/112982552/new-public-media-fund-to-boost-regional-news-coverage (accessed 31 July 2019).

52 Edmunds and Pullar-Strecker, 'Stuff to sell or close 28 community and rural newspapers'.

53 Tess McClure, 'Fighting the behemoth: Sustaining hyper-local public interest journalism in the digital age', Robert Bell Research Summary, 2017, p.7, www.canterbury.ac.nz/media/documents/postgraduate-/Tess-McClure-Robert-Bell-Report-Final.pdf (accessed 31 July 2019).

54 Jeremy Rose, 'The decline and fall of local body reporting', *Mediawatch*, Radio New Zealand, 2 December 2018, www.rnz.co.nz/national/programmes/mediawatch/audio/2018672853/the-decline-and-fall-of-local-body-reporting (accessed 31 July 2019).

55 Interview with Ian Telfer, 29 April 2017.

56 A 2009 survey found that 57 per cent of Dunedin residents over fifteen read the *Otago Daily Times* on an average day. Mark Derby, 'Newspapers', Te Ara – the Encyclopedia of New Zealand, http://www.TeAra.govt.nz/en/newspapers (accessed 14 August 2019).

57 Nielsen (ed.), *Local Journalism*.

58 Interview with Ian Telfer, 29 April 2017.

59 Wayne Hope, 'New thoughts on the public sphere in Aotearoa/New Zealand', in Hirst, Phelan and Rupar (eds), *Scooped*, pp.27–47.

60 Gavin Ellis, *Word War: How 125 Years of Newspaper Co-Operation Was Consigned to History*, VDM Verlag Dr. Müller, Saarbrücken, 2009.

61 Phone interview with Gavin Ellis, 21 April 2017.

62 'Radio NZ looking for more content-sharing deals', *Newsroom*, 13 June 2018, www.newsroom.co.nz/2018/06/13/119160/radio-nz-looking-for-more-content-sharing-deals (accessed 30 July 2019).

63 Sean Phelan and Thomas Owen, 'The Paradoxes of Media Globalization: On the Banal "World" of New Zealand Journalism', *International Journal of Communication*, 4 (2010), pp.27–53.

64 Donald Matheson, 'People like us: The cultural geography of New Zealand's international news', in Hirst, Phelan and Rupar (eds), *Scooped*, pp.128–40.

65 Ole R. Holsti, *Public Opinion and American Foreign Policy*, rev. edn, University of Michigan Press, Ann Arbor, MI, 2004.

66 Kyle Dropp, Joshua D. Kertzer and Thomas Zeitzoff, 'The less Americans know about Ukraine's location, the more they want U.S. to intervene', *Washington Post*, 7 April 2014, www. washingtonpost.com/news/ monkey-cage/wp/2014/04/07/ the-less-americans-know-about-ukraines-location-the-more-they-want-u-s-to-intervene/?utm_ term=.44910d1431b5 (accessed 20 May 2018).

67 Michael Gurevitch, Mark R. Levy and Itzhak Roeh, 'The global newsroom: Convergences and diversities in the globalization of television news', in Peter Dahlgren and Colin Sparks (eds), *Communications and Citizenship: Journalism and the Public Sphere in the New Media Age*, Routledge, London, 1991, pp.195–216.

68 Richard Sambrook, *Are Foreign Correspondents Redundant?: The Changing Face of International News*, Reuters Institute, Oxford, 2010.

69 They included major newswires, as well as BBC World Service, the *Washington Post*, the *Guardian* and Al Jazeera, and humanitarian specialists IRIN and the Thomson Reuters Foundation. See Martin Scott, Kate Wright and Mel Bunce, 'The state of humanitarian journalism', report, University of East Anglia, Norwich, October 2018, http://humanitarian-journalism.net/wp-content/uploads/2018/10/ Humanitarian-News-Report. pdf (accessed 2 January 2018).

70 Sara Vui-Talitu and Richard Pamatatau, 'Niu views on public broadcasting', in Johnson, Tiso, Illingworth and Bennett (eds), *Don't Dream It's Over*, p.41.

71 Laura Walters, 'Allow media to help shine a light on Pacific issues', *Newsroom*, 29 April 2019, www.newsroom. co.nz/2019/04/29/551732/ allow-media-to-help-shine-a-light-on-pacific-issues (accessed 13 August 2019).

72 Alan Rusbridger, *Breaking*

News: The Remaking of Journalism and Why It Matters Now, Canongate, London, 2018, p.xxiii.

73 Ibid., p.36.

74 Roy Greenslade retirement event, City, University of London, 22 May 2018.

75 Bernard Hickey, 'Key says after reports from TVNZ, RNZ and Hager on Panama Papers that Hager a "left wing conspiracy theorist"; says NZ just a "footnote" in latest revelations; says Govt may reform foreign trust if Shewan recommends', interest.co.nz, 9 May 2016, www.interest.co.nz/news/81470/key-says-after-reports-tvnz-rnz-and-hager-panama-papers-hager-left-wing-conspiracy (accessed 10 June 2018).

76 'Panama Papers: New Zealand to tighten trust laws after being named in leaks', ABC News, 13 July 2016, www.abc.net.au/news/2017-13/new-zealand-tightens-trust-laws-after-panama-papers/7625250 (accessed 20 July 2019). In a similar vein, at the launch of *Hit and Run* in 2017 (Nicky Hager and Jon Stephenson, *Hit and Run: The New Zealand SAS in Afghanistan and the Meaning of Honour*, Potton & Burton, Nelson, 2017), Mike Hosking told his listeners on Newstalk ZB: 'I have no time for the guy, I think he's a conspiratorialist and he's out to get the government … even if he has something this time, he comes with so much baggage, he's tarnished before he almost arrives.' Mike Hosking on *The Mike Hosking Breakfast*, Newstalk ZB, 22 March 2017.

77 Tim McKinnel, 'The real balance sheet', Public Address, 9 November 2015, https://publicaddress.net/speaker/the-real-balance-sheet (accessed 29 July 2019).

78 Dudding, 'Where now for TV current affairs?'.

79 McKinnel, 'The real balance sheet'.

80 Melanie Reid, 'NZ's own "taken generation"', *Newsroom*, 11 June 2019, www.newsroom.co.nz/@investigations/2019/06/11/629363/nzs-own-taken-generation (accessed 30 July 2019).

81 Colin Peacock, 'Baby uplift story raises awkward questions', *Mediawatch*, Radio New Zealand, 16 June 2019, www.rnz.co.nz/national/programmes/mediawatch/audio/2018699644/baby-uplift-story-raises-awkward-

questions (accessed 31 July 2019).

82   Pippa Norris, *A Virtuous Circle: Political Communications in Postindustrial Societies*, Cambridge University Press, Cambridge, 2000, p.29. As Onora O'Neill argued in her Reith Lecture: 'If powerful institutions are allowed to publish, circulate and promote material without indicating what is known and what is rumour; what is derived from a reputable source and what is invented, what is standard analysis and what is speculation; which sources may be knowledgeable and which are probably not, they damage our public culture and all our lives.' Onora O'Neill, 'A Question of Trust', The Reith Lectures, BBC, 2002, www.bbc.co.uk/programmes/p00ghvd8 (accessed 8 June 2018).

83   Nick Davies, *Flat Earth News: An Award-winning Reporter Exposes Falsehood, Distortion and Propaganda in the Global Media*, Vintage, London, 2009, p.59.

84   Helen Sissons, 'Negotiating the news: Interactions behind the curtain of the journalism–public relations relationship', *Journalism Studies*, 17, 2 (2016), pp.177–98, https://doi.org/10.1080/1461670X.2014.973147 (accessed 20 July 2019).

85   Erin McKenzie, 'Public relations vs journalism: Is the rise of PR a threat to the fourth estate?', *StopPress*, 1 December 2015, http://stoppress.co.nz/news/public-service-journalism-versus-public-relations-professionals-uprising-pr-threatening-fourth-estate (accessed 9 June 2018). These statistics may understate the situation because public relations officers sometimes call themselves consultants or 'journalists' to help maintain their professional identity, or to potentially obscure the strategic nature of their work. Phil Vine at Greenpeace, for example, describes himself as a 'journalist' while being employed by an NGO to advance its strategic causes. See Phil Vine, 'When is a journalist not a journalist? Negotiating a new form of advocacy journalism within the environmental movement', *Pacific Journalism Review*, 23, 1 (2017), https://doi.org/10.24135/pjr.v23i1.212 (accessed 20 July 2019).

86 This is sometimes referred to as 'strategic communication for social change'. Erica Ciszek's research on the 'It Gets Better' movement illustrates the overlap between activists and public relations groups: Erica Ciszek, 'Activist strategic communication for social change: A transnational case study of lesbian, gay, bisexual, and transgender activism', *Journal of Communication*, 67, 5 (2017), pp.702–18, https://doi.org/10.1111/jcom.12319 (accessed 20 July 2019).

87 For a discussion of these issues, see John Lloyd and Laura Toogood, *Journalism and PR: News Media and Public Relations in the Digital Age*, I. B. Tauris & Co. Ltd in association with the Reuters Institute, Oxford, 2015.

88 This is a particularly important feature of international reporting, where NGOs and their publicity teams will pay for journalists to travel with them to see a crisis zone – travel that the journalists could not afford or do safely by themselves. See, for example, Kate Wright, *Who's Reporting Africa Now?: Non-Governmental Organizations, Journalists,* *and Multimedia*, Peter Lang, Bern, 2018.

89 Richard Mulgan, *Politics in New Zealand*, 3rd edn, Auckland University Press, 2004, p.303.

90 Steve Maharey, 'Politicians as news sources', in J. McGregor (ed.), *Dangerous Democracy*, Dunmore Press, Palmerston North, 1995, p.97.

91 Margie Comrie, 'Politics, power and political journalists', in Hirst, Phelan and Rupar (eds), *Scooped*, p.119.

92 Phil Pennington, 'Government's public relations teams rapidly expanding', Radio New Zealand, 25 July 2019, www.rnz.co.nz/news/national/395107/government-s-public-relations-teams-rapidly-expanding (accessed 28 July 2019).

93 Ibid.

94 Marwick was talking to Colin Peacock on *Mediawatch* episode 'John Key's blogger ties remain in the dark', *Mediawatch*, Radio New Zealand, 26 March 2017, www.radionz.co.nz/national/programmes/mediawatch/audio/201836858/john-key's-blogger-ties-remain-in-the-dark (accessed 20 July 2019).

95 Colin Peacock, 'Getting it out

in the open: Reviewing the OIA', *Mediawatch*, Radio New Zealand, 8 November 2015, www.radionz.co.nz/national/programmes/mediawatch/audio/201777171/getting-it-out-in-the-open-reviewing-the-oia (accessed 21 January 2019).

96   Interview with Kirsty Johnston, Auckland, 8 May 2017.

97   Gavin Ellis, *Complacent Nation*, Bridget Williams Books, Wellington, 2016, https://doi.org/10.7810/9780947492946 (accessed 20 July 2019).

98   Naomi Oreskes and Erik Conway, *Merchants of Doubt*, Bloomsbury, London, 2010.

99   Nicky Hager, 'Twenty-five ways to have better journalism', in Hirst, Phelan and Rupar (eds), *Scooped*, pp.213–32.

100 Shaun Hendy, *Silencing Science*, Bridget Williams Books, 2016, p.36, https://doi.org/10.7810/9780947492847 (accessed 2 August 2019).

101 Asher Emanuel, 'Selling influence: Meet the lobbyists shaping New Zealand politics for a fee', *The Spinoff*, 12 February 2018, https://thespinoff.co.nz/politics/12-02-2018/meet-nzs-new-breed-of-political-lobbyists/ (accessed 20 July 2019).

102 Karl du Fresne, 'Burning issues', *New Zealand Listener*, 26 May 2017.

103 Petroc Sumner et al., 'The association between exaggeration in health related science news and academic press releases: Retrospective observational study', *British Medical Journal*, 349 (2014), g7015, https://doi.org/10.1136/bmj.g7015 (accessed 20 July 2019).

104 Denise-Marie Ordway, '53% of journalists surveyed weren't sure they could spot flawed research', Journalist's Resource, 29 July 2019, https://journalistsresource.org/studies/society/news-media/research-quality-news-annual-survey (accessed 31 July 2019).

105 Experienced prankster John Bohannon illustrated this vulnerability in 2015 when he fooled media outlets around the world with a fake study claiming that eating chocolate accelerates weight loss. Bohannon created a fake website, ran a mock trial and then sent out a press release. This was immediately republished, without question,

by news outlets in twenty countries, assisted by 'a small army of journalists who were either too stressed or too lazy to check the facts'. See Maria Godoy, 'Why a journalist scammed the media into spreading bad chocolate science', *NPR*, 28 May 2015, www.npr.org/sections/thesalt/2015/05/28/41031 3446/why-a-journalist-scammed-the-media-into-spreading-bad-chocolate-science (accessed 20 July 2019).

106 James Hollings (ed.), *A Moral Truth: 150 Years of Investigative Journalism in New Zealand*, Massey University Press, Auckland, 2017, p.329.

107 Keith Ng, 'MSD's leaky servers', *OnPoint*, Public Address, 14 October 2012, https://publicaddress.net/onpoint/msds-leaky-servers (accessed 20 July 2019).

108 'Melanie Reid: Investigative journalism', *Sunday Morning*, Radio New Zealand, 25 June 2017, www.rnz.co.nz/national/programmes/sunday/audio/201848765/melanie-reid-investigative-journalism (accessed 20 July 2019).

109 David Cohen, 'Judging the "immoderate" moderator', *National Business Review*, 25 August 2017.

110 Ibid., p.5. See also Sarah Sharp, 'Newspapers', in Janine Hayward and Chris Rudd (eds), *Political Communications in New Zealand*, Pearson Education, Auckland, 2004, p.117.

111 Joseph N. Cappella and Kathleen Hall Jamieson, *Spiral of Cynicism: The Press and the Public Good*, Oxford University Press, New York, NY, 1997.

112 Dannagal G. Young, 'Stop covering politics as a game', Nieman Lab, December 2017, www.niemanlab.org/2017/12/stop-covering-politics-as-a-game (accessed 31 July 2019).

113 Jürgen Habermas (trans. Thomas Burger), *The Structural Transformation of the Public Sphere: An Inquiry into a Category of Bourgeois Society*, Polity Press, Cambridge, 1989.

114 Max Rashbrooke, 'We need both tougher and gentler ways to get at the truth', *Scoop*, 25 October 2015, www.scoop.co.nz/stories/HL1510/S00053/we-need-both-tougher-and-gentler-ways-to-get-at-the-truth.htm (accessed 9 June 2018).

115 Richard Fletcher and Rasmus

Kleis Nielsen, 'Are people incidentally exposed to news on social media? A comparative analysis', *New Media & Society*, 20, 7 (2018), pp.2450–68, https://doi.org/10.1177%2F1461444817724170 (accessed 20 July 2019).

116 Richard Fletcher and Rasmus Kleis Nielsen, 'Automated serendipity: The effect of using search engines on news repertoire balance and diversity', *Digital Journalism*, 6, 8 (2018), pp.976–89, https://doi.org/10.1080/21670811.2018.1502045 (accessed 20 July 2019).

117 'Many Facebook users see political views that differ from their own', Pew Research Center, 20 October 2014, www.journalism.org/2014/10/21/political-polarization-media-habits/pj_14-10-21_mediapolarization-04 (accessed 1 August 2019).

118 Matthew Gentzkow and Jesse M. Shapiro, 'Ideological segregation online and offline', *Quarterly Journal of Economics*, 126, 4 (2011), pp.1799–839, https://doi.org/10.1093/qje/qjr044 (accessed 2 August 2019). See also Frederik J. Zuiderveen Borgesius et al., 'Should we worry about filter bubbles?', *Internet Policy Review*, 5, 1 (2016), https://doi.org/10.14763/2016.1.401 (accessed 2 August 2019).

119 This discussion focuses on the majority of average news consumers. It is important to acknowledge that there are a (small) number of more extreme news consumers who do go down 'worm holes' online. This has particularly been documented on YouTube, where the website's suggested videos can become more and more extreme. See Zeynep Tufekci, 'YouTube, the great radicalizer', *New York Times*, 10 March 2018, www.nytimes.com/2018/03/10/opinion/sunday/youtube-politics-radical.html (accessed 1 August 2019).

120 Fletcher and Nielsen, 'Automated serendipity'.

121 Michael A. Beam, Myiah J. Hutchens and Jay D. Hmielowski, 'Facebook news and (de)polarization: Reinforcing spirals in the 2016 US election', *Information, Communication & Society*, 21, 7 (2018), pp.940–58, https://doi.org/10.1080/1369118X.2018.1444783 (accessed 20 July 2019).

122 Augusto Valeriani and

Cristian Vaccari, 'Accidental exposure to politics on social media as online participation equalizer in Germany, Italy, and the United Kingdom', *New Media & Society*, 18, 9 (2016), pp.1857–74, https://doi.org/10.1177%2F1461444815616223 (accessed 20 July 2019).

123 Teun A. van Dijk, *Racism and the Press*, Routledge, London, 1991, p.20.

124 Jenny Rankine et al., 'Content and source analysis of newspaper items about Māori issues: Silencing the "natives" in Aotearoa?', *Pacific Journalism Review*, 20, 1 (2014), pp.213–33.

125 Ray Nairn et al., 'Māori news is bad news: That's certainly so on television', *MAI Journal*, 1, 1 (2012), pp.38–49, www.journal.mai.ac.nz/sites/default/files/MAI_Journal_v1%2C1_%20MoewakaBarnes_etal.pdf (accessed 20 July 2019).

126 See, for example, Sue Abel, *Shaping the News: Waitangi Day on Television*, Auckland University Press, 1997; Timothy McCreanor et al., 'The association of crime stories and Māori in Aotearoa New Zealand print media', *Sites: New Series*, 11, 1 (2014), pp.121–44, https://doi.org/10.11157/sites-vol1iss2id240 (accessed 20 July 2019); Ray Nairn et al., 'Māori news is bad news'.

127 Owen, 'Neocolonialism, nation-building and global journalism in Aotearoa', p.108.

128 Mihingarangi Forbes, 'Navigating the waters of Maori broadcasting', in Johnson, Tiso, Illingworth and Bennett (eds), *Don't Dream It's Over*, p.95.

129 Jo Smith, *Māori Television: The First Ten Years*, Auckland University Press, 2016, p.16.

130 Tapu Misa, 'Lifting our voices', *e-Tangata*, 3 March 2019, https://e-tangata.co.nz/media/lifting-our-voices (accessed 28 July 2019).

131 Robert Loto et al., 'Pasifika in the news: The portrayal of Pacific peoples in the New Zealand press', *Journal of Community and Applied Social Psychology*, 16, 2 (2006), pp.100–18, https://doi.org/10.1002/casp.848 (accessed 3 August 2019).

132 Sandra Kailahi, 'Pacificness – Telling our own side of the story', *Pacific Journalism Review*, 15, 1 (2009), pp.31–37; James Hollings, Folker Hanusch, Ravi Balasubramanian and Geoff Lealand, 'Causes for concern: The state of New Zealand

journalism in 2015', *Pacific Journalism Review*, 22, 2 (2016), pp.122–38.

133 Neil Thurman, Alessio Cornia and Jessica Kunert, 'Journalists in the UK', Reuters Institute, Oxford, 2015, https://reutersinstitute. politics.ox.ac.uk/sites/ default/files/research/files/ Journalists%2520in%2520 the%2520UK.pdf (accessed 20 July 2019).

134 Quoted in Sam Brett, 'Why would anyone train to be a journalist in NZ in 2019?' *The Spinoff*, 27 February 2019, https://thespinoff. co.nz/media/27-02-2019/ why-would-anyone-train-to- be-a-journalist-in-nz-in-2019 (accessed 30 July 2019).

135 Sue Abel, 'Māori, media and politics', in Geoff Kemp, Babak Bahador, Kate McMillan and Chris Rudd (eds), *Politics and the Media*, 2nd edn, Auckland University Press, 2016.

136 Nairn et al., 'Māori news is bad news'.

137 Michalia Arathimos, 'Ethnicity in the media', in Johnson, Tiso, Illingworth and Bennett (eds), *Don't Dream It's Over*, pp.237–46.

138 Abel, 'Māori, media and politics'.

139 Jenny Rankine et al., *Media and Te Tiriti o Waitangi 2007*, Kupu Taea, Auckland, 2007.

140 Aaron Smale, 'Media, Māori and me', *The Spinoff*, 30 March 2019, https://thespinoff.co.nz/ atea/30-03-2019/media- maori-and-me (accessed 4 April 2019).

141 'Why advertise on Māori Television', Māori Television, https://www.maoritelevision. com/about/sales-advertising/ why-advertise-maori- television (accessed 14 August 2019).

142 Mark Jennings, 'Māori TV's boo boo is over', *Newsroom*, 9 May 2017, www.newsroom. co.nz/2017/05/08/25675/ maori-tvs-boo-boo-is-over? utm_source=The+Bulletin &utm_campaign=1d9234c5e7- EMAIL_CAMPAIGN_2018_ 03_01_COPY_01&utm_ medium=email&utm_ term=0_552336e15a- 1d9234c5e7-533756713# (accessed 28 July 2019).

143 Te Puni Kōkiri, 'Impact of Māori Television on the Māori Language', Pārongo Fact Sheet 009–2011, July 2011, www.tpk.govt.nz/documents/ download/271/Impact- Survey-Maori-Television.pdf (accessed 10 June 2018).

144 Jessica Beaux Ormsby Paul, 'Māori perceptions of Māori

Television: An empirical study', Master's thesis, Auckland University of Technology, 2016.

145 Jo Smith and Sue Abel, 'Ka whawhai tonu mātou: Indigenous television in Aotearoa/New Zealand', *New Zealand Journal of Media Studies*, 11, 1 (2008), p.1, https://medianz.otago.ac.nz/medianz/article/viewFile/58/62 (accessed 20 July 2019).

146 Māori Television, 'Māori television marks fifth on-air anniversary', Throng, 26 March 2009, www.throng.co.nz/2009/03/Māori-television-marks-fifth-on-air-anniversary (accessed 29 August 2017).

147 Morgan Godfery, 'Against "political commentary"', in Johnson, Tiso, Illingworth and Bennett (eds), *Don't Dream It's Over*, p.281.

148 Wepiha Te Kanawa, 'Minister concerned about RNZ Māori content', *Te Ao Māori News*, 18 February 2016, https://teaomaori.news/minister-concerned-about-rnz-maori-content (accessed 28 July 2019).

149 Saziah Bashir, 'Saziah Bashir: Four things you should do following the Christchurch terror attacks', Radio New Zealand, 19 March 2019, www.rnz.co.nz/news/on-the-inside/385064/saziah-bashir-four-things-you-should-do-following-the-christchurch-terror-attacks (accessed 3 August 2019).

150 Edward W. Said, *Orientalism*, Pantheon Books, New York, 1978.

151 Saifuddin Ahmed and Jörg Matthes, 'Media representation of Muslims and Islam from 2000 to 2015: A meta-analysis', *International Communication Gazette*, 79, 3 (2017), pp.219–44, https://doi.org/10.1177/1748048516656305 (accessed 3 August 2019).

152 Kerry Moore, Paul Mason and Justin Lewis, 'Images of Islam in the UK: The Representation of British Muslims in the National Print News Media 2000–2008', Cardiff School of Journalism, Media and Cultural Studies, 7 July 2008, www.channel4.com/news/media/pdfs/Cardiff%20Final%20Report.pdf (accessed 3 August 2019).

153 Khairiah A. Rahman and A. Emadi, 'Representations of Islam and Muslims in New Zealand media', *Pacific Journalism Review*, 24, 2 (2018), pp.166–88, https://doi.

org/10.24135/pjr.v24i2.419 (accessed 3 August 2019).

154 Derek Cheng, 'Media blamed for Islam's image', *New Zealand Herald*, 21 July 2005, www.nzherald.co.nz/nz/news/article.cfm?c_id=1&objectid=10336831 (accessed 3 August 2019).

155 Whitney Phillips, *The Oxygen of Amplification: Better Practices for Reporting on Extremists, Antagonists, and Manipulators*, Executive Summary, Data & Society Research Institute, 22 May 2018, https://datasociety.net/output/oxygen-of-amplification (accessed 30 July 2019).

156 Not everyone agrees the underlying ideology should be sidelined in reports; some argue that it's important to also dissect these ideas and the process of radicalisation. Where most people agree, however, is that there should not be 'celebrity-style profiles' of the shooters or any reproduction of hateful ideology without context or critique. See also Mathew Ingram, 'New Zealand massacre: Journalists divided on how to cover hate', *Columbia Journalism Review*, 15 March 2019, www.cjr.org/the_new_gatekeepers/new-zealand-shooting-christchurch.php (accessed 30 July 2019).

157 For example, the New Zealand shooter mentioned mass murderers in Charleston, South Carolina, as well as a Norwegian murderer who killed sixty-nine political activists and children at a summer camp. Jason Baumgartner et al., 'What we learned from analyzing thousands of stories on the Christchurch shooting', *Columbia Journalism Review*, 26 March 2019, www.cjr.org/analysis/christchurch-shooting-media-coverage.php (accessed 30 July 2019).

158 Ibid.

159 'Christchurch mosque shootings: The faces of the victims', *New Zealand Herald*, 16 March 2019, www.nzherald.co.nz/nz/news/article.cfm?c_id=1&objectid=12213358 (accessed 3 August 2019).

160 Farzana Noorzai and Toni Bruce, 'NZ media shows world high-quality coverage of Islam', *Newsroom*, 28 March 2019, www.newsroom.co.nz/@ideasroom/2019/03/28/508794/nz-media-shows-world-high-quality-coverage-of-islam# (accessed 30 July 2019).

161 'Broadcaster Chris Lynch apologises for anti-islamic column', Stuff, 20 March 2019, www.stuff.co.nz/national/christchurch-shooting/111423439/broadcaster-chris-lynch-apologises-for-antiislamic-column (accessed 1 August 2019).

162 Rachel Smalley, 'Rachel Smalley: Diversity in prime time fundamental', Newstalk ZB, 10 August 2015, www.newstalkzb.co.nz/on-air/early-edition/opinion/rachel-smalley-diversity-in-prime-time-fundamental (accessed 31 July 2019).

163 Hollings et al., 'Causes for concern'; 'NZ: Journalists working harder, women disadvantaged, says new PJR research', Pacific Media Centre, 28 February 2017, www.pmc.aut.ac.nz/pacific-media-watch/nz-journalists-working-harder-women-disadvantaged-says-new-pjr-research-9817 (accessed 9 June 2018).

164 Godfery, 'Against "political commentary"', p.280. See also Rankine et al., 'Content and source analysis of newspaper items about Māori issues'. The authors find that male sources outnumber female two to one.

165 Ed Grover, 'Research reveals proportion of women in flagship broadcast news shows', City, University of London, 20 May 2016, www.city.ac.uk/news/2016/may/new-research-reveals-proportion-of-women-experts,-reporters-and-presenters-in-the-news (accessed 9 June 2018).

166 Tim Murphy, 'Time to wipe the cultural sleep from our eyes', Newsroom, 14 April 2017, www.newsroom.co.nz/2017/04/13/19051/e-tangata (accessed 21 January 2019).

167 Lauren Ober, '57 black-hosted podcasts you should probably listen to', Medium, 14 July 2016, https://medium.com/@oberandout/56-black-hosted-podcasts-that-you-should-probably-listen-to-510456b6465f (accessed 29 July 2019).

168 See, for example, Alex Casey and Hayden Donnell, 'This article about terrible millennials is quite sexist and dumb', The Spinoff, 16 June 2016, http://thespinoff.co.nz/media/16-06-2016/this-article-about-terrible-millennials-is-quite-sexist-and-dumb (accessed 15 June 2018). See also Alex Casey,

'Why the AM Show has got me in a tizzy', *The Spinoff*, 16 August 2017, https://thespinoff.co.nz/tv/16-08-2017/why-the-am-show-has-got-me-in-a-tizzy (accessed 15 June 2018).

169 Mel Bunce, 'International news and the image of Africa: New storytellers, new narratives?', in Julia Gallagher (ed.), *Images of Africa: Creation, Negotiation and Subversion*, Manchester University Press, 2015. Another great example is the website 'Africa is a Country' – this started as the website of a sole academic, and has grown into a major platform with a team of editors and over 500 contributors who have helped change the debate around the representation of Africa.

170 The hashtag #BobJonesIsA Racist trended on Twitter in June 2018, for example, as part of a backlash against Sir Bob Jones's media comments about Māori. There was also a strong backlash on Twitter in response to the *New Zealand Herald* article 'One week, three kids ... how hard can it be?' (Greg Bruce, 9 June 2018), which suggested that women were the primary caregivers, and men were 'playing a role' when they looked after their kids. One tweet from Hilary Barry mocking the cover received more than 2,500 likes: probably more attention on Twitter than original *Herald* article received.

171 Andrew Chadwick, *The Hybrid Media System: Politics and Power*, Oxford University Press, Oxford, 2013.

172 Becky Gardiner et al., 'The dark side of Guardian comments', *Guardian*, 12 April 2016, www.theguardian.com/technology/2016/apr/12/the-dark-side-of-guardian-comments (accessed 9 June 2018).

173 You can watch Anita Sarkeesian discuss these issues in her TEDx Talk from 2012, www.youtube.com/watch?v=GZAxwsg9J9Q (accessed 20 July 2019).

174 Kevin Rawlinson, 'Labour MP calls for end to online anonymity after "600 rape threats"', *Guardian*, 11 June 2018, www.theguardian.com/society/2018/jun/11/labour-mp-jess-phillips-calls-for-end-to-online-anonymity-after-600-threats (accessed 14 June 2018).

175 Mary Beard, *Women & Power: A Manifesto*, Profile Books, London, 2017.

176 For a good discussion, see Morgan Godfery, 'Burn the witch: On the attacks against Eleanor Catton', *Overland*, 29 January 2015, https://overland.org.au/2015/01/on-the-attacks-against-eleanor-catton (accessed 10 June 2018).

177 Paulette Benton-Greig, Dhakshi Gamage and Nicola Gavey, 'Doing and denying sexism: Online responses to a New Zealand feminist campaign against sexist advertising', *Feminist Media Studies*, 18, 3 (2018), pp.349–65, https://doi.org/10.1080/14680777.2017.1367703 (accessed 20 July 2019).

178 Megan Whelan, 'Gender bias and Facebook comments: Is there a male equivalent of a vile hag?', Radio New Zealand, 4 May 2017, www.radionz.co.nz/news/top/330011/facebook-comments-is-there-a-male-equivalent-of-a-vile-hag (accessed 6 June 2018).

179 Whelan was speaking at the event 'More Than a Pretty Face – 4 Women under 40 Talk Politics', City Gallery, Wellington, 24 August 2017.

180 Charlotte Graham-McLay, '"Why do I have to put up with this shit?" Women journalists in NZ share their stories of online abuse', *The Spinoff*, 6 September 2017, https://thespinoff.co.nz/media/06-09-2017/why-do-i-have-to-put-up-with-this-shit-women-journalists-in-nz-share-their-stories-of-online-abuse (accessed 5 June 2018).

181 Catherine Adams, 'Female technology journalists report abuse is still the name of the game', *Guardian*, 11 October 2015, www.theguardian.com/media/2015/oct/11/female-technology-journalists-abuse-zoe-quinn (accessed 5 June 2018).

Chapter 4

1   NZ on Screen, *Tonight – Robert Muldoon interview*, 1976, www.nzonscreen.com/title/tonight-muldoon-interview-1976 (accessed 14 June 2018).

2   Māori Television, *All Talk with Anika Moa – Series 2, Episode 7*, 14 June 2017, www.Māoritelevision.com/tv/shows/all-talk-anika-moa/S02E007/all-talk-anika-moa-series-2-episode-7 (accessed 11 June 2018).

3   Surveys show that the number of young people reading newspapers in industrialised countries has been declining for several decades – from

long before the internet was introduced. This is not linked to the readers' 'stage of life': younger groups are not starting to read more newspapers as they age (which may have been the case historically). See, for example, Wolfram Peiser, 'Cohort replacement and the downward trend in newspaper readership', *Newspaper Research Journal*, 21, 2 (2000), pp.11–22, https://doi.org/10.1177%2F073953290002100202 (accessed 20 July 2019); Edmund Lauf, 'Research note: The vanishing young reader: Sociodemographic determinants of newspaper use as a source of political information in Europe, 1980–98', *European Journal of Communication*, 16, 2 (2001), pp.233–43, https://doi.org/10.1177%2F0267323101016002005 (accessed 20 July 2019); Carol Schlagheck, 'Newspaper reading choices by college students', *Newspaper Research Journal*, 19, 2 (1998), pp.74–87, https://doi.org/10.1177%2F073953299801900206 (accessed 20 July 2019); George L. Thurlow and Katherine J. Milo,

'Newspaper readership: Can the bleeding be stopped, or do we have the wrong patient?', *Newspaper Research Journal*, 14, 3–4 (1993), pp.34–44, https://doi.org/10.1177%2F073953299301400305 (accessed 20 July 2019).

4 Lauf, 'Research note'.

5 This compares to 39 per cent of those fifty and above. Equally dramatically, only 38 per cent of this younger group watch TV news daily, as opposed to a whopping 87 per cent of the older group. Katerina Eva Matsa, Elisa Shearer, Mason Walker and Laura Silver, 'Western Europeans under 30 view news media less positively, rely more on digital platforms than older adults', Pew Research Center, 30 October 2018, www.journalism.org/2018/10/30/western-europeans-under-30-view-news-media-less-positively-rely-more-on-digital-platforms-than-older-adults (accessed 8 January 2018). See also Ofcom, 'News consumption in the UK: 2018', produced by Jigsaw Research, www.ofcom.org.uk/__data/assets/pdf_file/0024/116529/news-consumption-2018.pdf (accessed 8 January 2018).

6 When eighteen- to twenty-

nine-year-olds want news, they go online: 73 per cent got news from the internet 'at least daily', as opposed to the 48 per cent of those aged fifty and above. And although they don't read newspapers in print, younger Europeans do consume, rely on and trust newspaper brands online. Although it's worth noting that people who read newspapers online do not necessarily spend long doing so. Neil Thurman, who researches news consumption patterns, assessed 'time spent' on websites and found that, typically, a UK national newspaper brand will get an average of 40 minutes of reading time per user per day on its print papers, but just 30 seconds per user per day on its website and apps. Neil Thurman, 'Newspaper consumption in the mobile age: Re-assessing multi-platform performance and market share using "time-spent"', *Journalism Studies*, 19, 10 (2018), pp.1409–29, http://dx.doi.org/10.1080/146167 0X.2017.1279028 (accessed 20 July 2019).

7   Alan Rusbridger, *Breaking News: The Remaking of Journalism and Why It Matters*

Now, Canongate, London, 2018, p.306.

8   Newsprint will likely last the longest at prestige, feature and lifestyle outlets. When we read for pleasure, diversion, or deep dives, the speed of the delivery is less important, and the experience is more so.

9   Rusbridger, *Breaking News*, p.29.

10   WAN-IFRA, 'World Press Trends 2018: Measuring the value of trust', 2018, https://blog.wan-ifra.org/2018/10/02/available-now-world-press-trends-2018-measuring-the-value-of-trust (accessed 20 July 2019).

11   David Williams, 'The future of newspapers', *Newsroom*, 8 January 2018, www.newsroom.co.nz/@summer-newsroom/2018/01/07/72973/the-future-of-newspapers (accessed 7 January 2019).

12   As Mark Derby notes, New Zealand's five main dailies remained confined to their own geographical areas, with little overlapping readership. This regional character has helped to sustain the newspapers in the face of competition from other media and from each other. Mark Derby, 'Newspapers', Te Ara – the Encyclopedia of

New Zealand, http://www.
TeAra.govt.nz/en/newspapers
(accessed 14 August 2019).

13 Roy Greenslade, 'Last
chance to fill in the blanks on
funding journalism's future',
Guardian, 1 July 2018, www.
theguardian.com/media/
media-blog/2018/jul/01/
journalism-funding-future-
press (accessed 8 January
2018). Clay Shirky, who has
predicted and explained
many digital transformations,
echoes this statement, noting
that 'many of [newsprint's]
most passionate defenders
are unable, even now, to
plan for a world in which the
industry they knew is visibly
going away'. Clay Shirky,
'Newspapers and thinking
the unthinkable', 13 March
2009, www.shirky.com/
weblog/2009/03/newspapers-
and-thinking-the-unthinkable
(accessed 21 January 2019).

14 Alex S. Jones, *Losing the News:
The Future of the News that
Feeds Democracy*, Oxford
University Press, Oxford,
2009.

15 Rasmus Kleis Nielsen, 'A long
slow slog with no one coming
to the rescue', Nieman Lab,
January 2019, www.niemanlab.
org/2019/01/a-long-slow-slog-
with-no-one-coming-to-the-
rescue (accessed 21 January
2019).

16 Ibid.

17 Jesse Mulligan with Anusha
Bradley, 'Blood from a stone:
Getting local councils to
comment', *Afternoons with
Jesse Mulligan*, Radio New
Zealand, 7 August 2019,
www.rnz.co.nz/national/
programmes/afternoons/
audio/2018707618/blood-
from-a-stone-getting-
local-councils-to-comment
(accessed 14 August 2019).

18 Stephanie Peatling, 'ABC most
trusted news source, poll
shows, after Turnbull minister
accuses it of "fake news"',
Sydney Morning Herald, 23
December 2016, www.smh.
com.au/politics/federal/abc-
most-trusted-news-source-
poll-shows-after-turnbull-
minister-accuses-it-of-fake-
news-20161222-gtgmqa.html
(accessed 9 June 2018).

19 John Plunkett, 'BBC News
most trusted source for more
than half of people in the UK',
Guardian, 10 March 2016, www.
theguardian.com/media/2016/
mar/10/bbc-news-most-
trusted-source-for-more-
than-half-of-people-in-the-uk
(accessed 9 June 2016).

20 See the full report: Michael
W. Kearney, 'Trusting News

Project Report 2017: A Reynolds Journalism Institute research project', 25 July 2017, www.rjionline.org/reporthtml.html (accessed 9 June 2018).

21 BBC, 'Local News Partnerships: Local Democracy Reporting Service', 2019, www.bbc.com/lnp/ldrs (accessed 20 July 2019).

22 'In Britain, a team effort to help local news survive', *New York Times*, 9 December 2018, www.nytimes.com/2018/12/09/business/bbc-local-news-partnership.html (accessed 20 July 2019).

23 Charlotte Tobitt, 'BBC-funded local democracy reporters filed 50,000 stories in first year with nearly all roles filled', *PressGazette*, 17 January 2019, www.pressgazette.co.uk/bbc-funded-local-democracy-reporters-filed-50000-stories-in-first-year-with-nearly-all-roles-filled (accessed 17 January 2019).

24 Ibid.

25 Colin Peacock, 'New collaboration puts reporters in the regions but future funding is already in doubt', *Mediawatch*, Radio New Zealand, 2 June 2019, www.rnz.co.nz/national/programmes/mediawatch/audio/2018697564/new-collaboration-puts-reporters-in-the-regions-but-future-funding-is-already-in-doubt (accessed 14 August 2019).

26 NZ On Air, 'NZ On Air and RNZ launch new Local Democracy Reporting', press release, 27 May 2019, www.scoop.co.nz/stories/PO1905/S00391/nz-on-air-and-rnz-launch-new-local-democracy-reporting.htm (accessed 28 July 2019).

27 Tess McClure, 'Fighting the behemoth: Sustaining hyper-local public interest journalism in the digital age', Robert Bell Research Summary, 2017, p.36, www.canterbury.ac.nz/media/documents/postgraduate-/Tess-McClure-Robert-Bell-Report-Final.pdf (accessed 31 July 2019).

28 Claire Wardle, 'Fake news. It's complicated', *First Draft*, 16 February 2017, https://firstdraftnews.org/fake-news-complicated (accessed 10 June 2018).

29 For a helpful discussion of this, see John Cook, Stephan Lewandowsky and Ullrich Ecker, 'Neutralizing misinformation through inoculation: Exposing misleading argumentation techniques reduces their influence', *PLoS ONE*, 12, 5 (2017), pp.1–21, https://

doi.org/10.1371/journal. pone.0175799 (accessed 20 July 2019).

30 Hugo Mercier and Dan Sperber, *The Enigma of Reason*, Harvard University Press, Cambridge, MA, 2017.

31 Cited in Elizabeth Kolbert, 'Why facts don't change our minds: New discoveries about the human mind show the limitations of reason', *New Yorker*, 19 February 2017, www.newyorker.com/ magazine/2017/02/27/why-facts-dont-change-our-minds (accessed 5 June 2018).

32 Brendan Nyhan and Jason Reifler, 'When corrections fail: The persistence of political misperceptions', *Political Behavior*, 32, 2 (2010), pp.303–30, www.jstor.org/ stable/40587320 (accessed 20 July 2019).

33 Ibid.

34 Jonas De keersmaecker and Arne Roets, '"Fake news": Incorrect, but hard to correct. The role of cognitive ability on the impact of false information on social impressions', *Intelligence*, 65 (2017), pp.107–10, http://hdl. handle.net/1854/LU-8541505 (accessed 20 July 2019).

35 Cuihua Shen et al., 'Fake images: The effects of source, intermediary, and digital media literacy on contextual assessment of image credibility online', *New Media & Society* (online first, 2018), pp.1–26, https://doi. org/10.1177%2F146144 4818799526 (accessed 20 July 2019).

36 Ibid., p.21.

37 See the project's website: Informed Health Choices, www. informedhealthchoices.org (accessed 10 June 2018).

38 Emma Charlton, 'How Finland is fighting fake news – in the classroom', World Economic Forum, 21 May 2019, www. weforum.org/agenda/2019/05/ how-finland-is-fighting-fake-news-in-the-classroom (accessed 4 August 2019).

39 'Quashing fake news with media literacy', California News Publishers Association, 16 March 2018, https://cnpa. com/quashing-fake-news-with-media-literacy (accessed 14 June 2018).

40 European Commission, 'Final report of the High Level Expert Group on Fake News and Online Disinformation', Directorate-General for Communication Networks, Content and Technology, 12 March 2018, https://ec.europa.eu/digital-single-market/en/news/

final-report-high-level-expert-group-fake-news-and-online-disinformation (accessed 15 June 2018).

41 'Fake news and how to spot it to be taught in schools', *Newsround*, BBC, 15 July 2019, www.bbc.co.uk/newsround/48988778 (accessed 28 July 2019).

42 Ed Grover, 'Research reveals proportion of women in flagship broadcast news shows', City, University of London, 20 May 2016, www.city.ac.uk/news/2016/may/new-research-reveals-proportion-of-women-experts,-reporters-and-presenters-in-the-news (accessed 9 June 2018).

43 A more radical approach to the issue of the pay gap, which has been introduced in the UK, is to make large companies publish the pay gap between their male and female employees. The organisations that don't want to look bad – or which are competing for the very best female employees – are directly incentivised to consider their company culture and policies, and think creatively about how to attract, support, keep and promote women.

44 Jim Waterson, 'Financial Times tool warns if articles quote too many men', *Guardian*, 14 November 2018, www.theguardian.com/media/2018/nov/14/financial-times-tool-warns-if-articles-quote-too-many-men (accessed 20 July 2019).

45 Cory L. Armstrong, 'The influence of reporter gender on source selection in newspaper stories', *Journalism & Mass Communication Quarterly*, 81, 1 (2004), pp.139–54, https://doi.org/10.1177%2F107769900408100110 (accessed 20 July 2019).

46 Nikki Usher, Jesse Holcomb and Justin Littman, 'Twitter makes it worse: Political journalists, gendered echo chambers, and the amplification of gender bias', *The International Journal of Press/Politics*, 23, 3 (2018), pp.324–44, https://doi.org/10.1177%2F1940161218781254 (accessed 20 July 2019).

47 Louise North, 'Still a "blokes club": The motherhood dilemma in journalism', *Journalism*, 17, 3 (2016), pp.315–30, https://doi.org/10.1177%2F1464884914560306 (accessed 20 July 2019).

48 Charlotte Graham-McLay, '"Why do I have to put up with this shit?" Women

journalists in NZ share their stories of online abuse', *The Spinoff*, 6 September 2017, https://thespinoff.co.nz/media/06-09-2017/why-do-i-have-to-put-up-with-this-shit-women-journalists-in-nz-share-their-stories-of-online-abuse (accessed 5 June 2018).

49 '"Informing is not a crime" UN chief calls for better protection of journalists, press freedom', *UN News*, 25 February 2019, https://news.un.org/en/story/2019/02/1033552 (accessed 4 August 2019).

50 'Media freedom and journalists under threat: Foreign Secretary's speech', speech by Rt Hon Jeremy Hunt MP, UK Foreign Secretary, Global Conference for Media Freedom, London, 10 July 2019, www.gov.uk/government/speeches/media-freedom-and-journalists-under-threat-foreign-secretarys-speech (4 August 2019).

51 Clooney was speaking during the plenary session: 'Defining media freedom and why it is important', speech by Amal Clooney, Global Conference for Media Freedom, London, 11 July 2019. See full videos of all the sessions at www.gov.uk/government/news/global-conference-for-media-freedom-london-2019-watch-live (accessed 27 July 2019).

52 Nic Newman et al., *Reuters Institute Digital News Report 2019*, Reuters Institute, Oxford, 2019, https://reutersinstitute.politics.ox.ac.uk/sites/default/files/2019-06/DNR_2019_FINAL_1.pdf (accessed 29 July 2019).

53 'Cameroon: Anatomy of a Killing – Documentary – BBC Africa Eye', YouTube, www.youtube.com/watch?v=XbnLkc6r3yc (accessed 5 August 2019). The Cameroon Government was forced to act, arresting the suspected killers – members of its own army.

54 Muhammad Idrees Ahmad, 'Bellingcat and how open source reinvented investigative journalism', *New York Review of Books*, 10 June 2019, www.nybooks.com/daily/2019/06/10/bellingcat-and-how-open-source-reinvented-investigative-journalism (accessed 5 August 2019).

55 Chris Anderson, 'New money, new mission', *The European*, 27 January 2013, www.theeuropean-magazine.com/chris-anderson/6346-journalism-as-a-public-good (accessed 9 June 2018).

ACKNOWLEDGEMENTS

A deep and sincere thank you to all who spoke with me as I was developing the ideas in this book.

I'd like to thank the many editors, former editors and journalists working across print, radio, TV and digital start-ups all around the country, particularly Sheila Byrne (Māori Television), Gavin Ellis (former editor, *New Zealand Herald*), Karl du Fresne (former editor, *Dominion Post*), Nicky Hager (investigative journalist), Bernard Hickey (*Newsroom*), Kirsty Johnston (*New Zealand Herald*), Toby Manhire (*The Spinoff*), Kate Newton (Radio New Zealand), Colin Peacock (Radio New Zealand), Jeremy Rose (Radio New Zealand), Philip Somerville (*Otago Daily Times*), Barry Stewart (Editor, *Otago Daily Times*), Ian Telfer (Radio New Zealand) and Megan Whelan (Radio New Zealand). But please note that, unless specifically quoted, this book does not reflect their views.

My heartfelt thanks also to the media commentators and researchers who spoke with me, including Bryce Edwards (Victoria University of Wellington), James Hollings (Massey University), Donald Matheson (University of Canterbury), Merja Myllylahti (Auckland University of Technology), Rasmus Nielsen (Oxford University), Sean Phelan (Massey University), Chris Rudd (University of Otago), Helen Sissons (AUT) and Peter Thompson (VUW).

ABOUT THE AUTHOR

Mel Bunce is a Reader in Journalism at City, University of London where she researches and teaches on the international news media. Dunedin-born, Mel worked as a columnist for the *Otago Daily Times* while she was a student at the University of Otago. After graduating, she won a Commonwealth Scholarship to the University of Oxford where she completed an MPhil in Development Studies, and a Doctorate in Politics. Mel is the coeditor of *Africa's Media Image in the 21st Century* (Routledge, 2016), and has published a number of research articles on international journalism.

About BWB Texts

BWB Texts are short books on big subjects from great New Zealand writers. They are succinct narratives spanning contemporary issues, memoir, history and science. With well over fifty BWB Texts in print and more available digitally, new works are published regularly. BWB Texts can be purchased from all good bookstores and online from www.bwb.co.nz.

BWB Texts include:

A Careful Revolution
David Hall

The Health of the People
David Skegg

Still Counting
Marilyn Waring

Maui Street
Morgan Godfery

Mountains to Sea
Mike Joy (ed.)

Ko Taranaki Te Maunga
Rachel Buchanan

False Divides
Lana Lopesi

A Matter of Fact: Talking Truth in a Post-Truth World
Jess Berentson-Shaw

Better Lives: Migration, Wellbeing and New Zealand
Julie Fry and Peter Wilson

Doing Our Bit: The Campaign to Double the Refugee Quota
Murdoch Stephens

Thought for Food: Why What We Eat Matters
John D. Potter

Island Time: New Zealand's Pacific Futures
Damon Salesa

Portacom City: Reporting on the Christchurch and Kaikōura Earthquakes
Paul Gorman

The Ground Between: Navigating the Oil and Mining Debate in New Zealand
Sefton Darby

Sea Change: Climate Politics and New Zealand
Bronwyn Hayward

The Best of e-Tangata
Edited by Tapu Misa and Gary Wilson

Antibiotic Resistance: The End of Modern Medicine?
Siouxsie Wiles

Hopes Dashed?: The Economics of Gender Inequality
Prue Hyman

Safeguarding the Future: Governing in an Uncertain World
Jonathan Boston

The Stolen Island: Searching for 'Ata
Scott Hamilton

The Post-Snowden Era: Mass Surveillance and Privacy in New Zealand
Kathleen Kuehn

The Bike and Beyond: Life on Two Wheels in Aotearoa New Zealand
Laura Williamson

Late Love: Sometimes Doctors Need Saving as Much as Their Patients
Glenn Colquhoun

Three Cities: Seeking Hope in the Anthropocene
Rod Oram

Playing for Both Sides: Love Across the Tasman
Stephanie Johnson

Complacent Nation
Gavin Ellis

**The First Migration: Māori Origins 3000BC –
AD1450**
Atholl Anderson

Silencing Science
Shaun Hendy

**Going Places: Migration, Economics and the
Future of New Zealand**
Julie Fry and Hayden Glass

The Interregnum: Rethinking New Zealand
Morgan Godfery (ed.)

Christchurch Ruptures
Katie Pickles

**Home Truths: Confronting New Zealand's
Housing Crisis**
Philippa Howden-Chapman

**Polluted Inheritance: New Zealand's Freshwater
Crisis**
Mike Joy

Wealth and New Zealand
Max Rashbrooke